Bible *Cameos*

80 Brief Biographies of Bible Characters

Ivor Powell

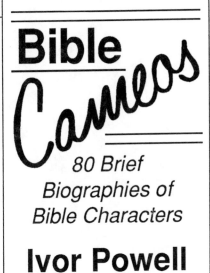

Bible Cameos

80 Brief Biographies of Bible Characters

Ivor Powell

Foreword by
G. Brand van Zyl

KREGEL PUBLICATIONS
Grand Rapids, Michigan 49501

Bible Cameos, by Ivor Powell. © 1951 by Ivor Powell. Published in 1985 by Kregel Publications, a division of Kregel, Inc., P. O. Box 2607, Grand Rapids, Michigan 49501.

Cover Design: Don Ellens
Cover Photo: Sid Lenger

Library of Congress Cataloging-in-Publication Data

Powell, Ivor, 1910-
  Bible Cameos.

      p.   cm.
  Reprint. Originally published: London: Marshall, Morgan & Scott, 1951.
  Includes index.
  1. Bible—Biography. I. Title.
BS571.P675   1985   220.9'2   84-23535
                                                          CIP
ISBN   0-8254-3515-3

        3 4 5 6 7 Printing/Year 95 94 93 92 91

CONTENTS

FOREWORD

The Rev. Ivor Powell, popularly known throughout South Africa as " The man from Wales," has laboured among our people, white, coloured and black, for three and a half years. His vivid representation of Bible scenes has attracted very large audiences to the services, and it is a stimulating thought that this interest has never wavered even though the crusades have extended over such a lengthy period. Mr. Powell is now to supply in book form his portraits of the old Bible characters, and I feel sure that all who have read his former volumes will await with eager anticipation the messages contained in " Bible Cameos." In these days of strain and tension the thoughts of mankind are turning again to the Scriptures, for there alone can strength be found for present-day requirements. I commend Mr. Powell's new book, and feel sure it will help all its readers.

RT. HON. G. BRAND VAN ZYL, P.C.
(Governor-General of South Africa, 1945-1950 Cape Town)

PREFACE

I think the idea of " Bible Cameos " first came to my mind during one of my earliest visits to Glasgow. At the close of a service, an eminent Christian surgeon said, " Mr. Powell, why don't you write something to help men like me? I love to preach the Gospel on Sundays, but during the week I am so busy attending to my patients that I have no time in which to study. When Saturday night comes, I find it so difficult to prepare a message for Sunday. Sir, why don't you write something to help fellows like me? " His request has often been repeated by other people during the years that have followed.

Then I shall always remember my eight years' pastorate in Wales, where the experience of having to prepare four and sometimes five messages each week taught me to understand the strain under which many young men begin their life-work. My long tour through Southern Africa brought me into vital contact with student ministers who were experiencing a similar difficulty, and their requests for this book could not be denied. I have therefore written a simple analysis of the leading Bible characters, and have modelled all the chapters on the pattern used in my evangelistic addresses. No minister wishes to preach another man's sermon, but we all freely acknowledge the help we receive from other men. I have, I trust, said enough to stimulate thought, and yet insufficient to form a sermon. Upon these meagre outlines, preachers will be able to formulate their own messages. Bible Cameos will supply a ready-made list of subjects for sermons, Bible classes, or special meetings, and it is my earnest prayer that these brief studies will help all my fellow ministers, whose help and comradeship I have found to be indispensable. I gratefully acknowledge the kindness of the Rt. Hon. G. Brand van Zyl, P.C., who has written the Foreword to this book. He was Governor-General of South Africa during most of my stay in that lovely land, and both he and Mrs. van Zyl attended my meetings in Pretoria. I still treasure the letters of appreciation which they sent to me from Government House.

A cameo is a small photographic jewel, and I have used that term in the title of the book because it seems to be the best way to express my thoughts concerning the great Bible portraits which I have tried to reproduce in smaller size. The concluding chapter, " Hints for the young preacher," should be read by all students, for there I have tried to express all the outstanding discoveries in my twenty years of preaching God's Gospel.

IVOR POWELL

BIBLE CAMEOS

ADAM . . . whose confidence went to bits

This modern world is a wonderful place. The motor-car, telephone, radio, and television are all milestones in the onward march of civilization. If the ancients could survive the shock of a return, they would probably have a most interesting time. Yet, when they had studied all the changes, they would shake their wise old heads and say, "Some things are unaltered. Man, his need, and his God, are just the same. As it was with Adam, so it is now."

Man Confident.

Poor Adam! His face is radiant. He has just accomplished his first great deed, and he is satisfied. For a little while he had been disturbed. Nakedness—horrid thought! —had upset his tranquil world. Mercilessly, it had arrived to wreck his buoyant innocence. Something was wrong, and Adam frowned. But man, ever resourceful, had found a way out of his dilemma. Ingenuity had woven a covering, and the need had been met. He put on his garment, and proudly surveyed the result. Yes, it was very nice. "Eve, you've done a grand job. Congratulations."

Poor Adam! He only succeeded in making a road along which all his children have since walked. With shining eyes and contented heart, he believed all was well. His desire to improve himself had been eminently successful. He smiled and patted himself on the back.

Ah, modern man, you are so like your father. You are so slow to learn that the greatness of human achievement can never atone for sin. Success in business, comfort at home, popularity among friends, can never clothe a naked soul. A modern villa is a poor substitute for an abiding place in the affections of God. Increasing worldly wealth can never compare with the untold riches of a divine smile.

Man Confounded.

Poor Adam! He's listening, and his smile has gone. Eve stands with her man, and trembles. "And they heard the voice of the Lord God walking in the garden in the cool of the day: and Adam and his wife hid themselves from the presence of the Lord God amongst the trees of the garden." Unfortunate man! In the moments which followed, he

1

made three startling discoveries. (i) *How inadequate his clothing*—he was still naked. (ii) *How inadequate his hiding place*—he could not evade God. (iii) *How inadequate his excuses*—he was still guilty. "Oh dear, why did God come to spoil everything? I was so happy until His voice sounded. My garments seemed perfectly satisfactory until —yes, until He came."

Adam, your children haven't changed. Conviction never reaches a soul until God speaks. We are blissfully content until the Lord God comes down to walk in the cool of our day; and then a tremor shakes our soul. Our virtuous deeds sink as the sun in the sky, and the shadows of doubt fill our horizon. Then we also would seek a hiding place, but alas, our world is so small.

Man Clothed

"The woman thou gavest me. She . . ." Sh! Adam. Be a man, and stand on your own feet. Don't blame another. Shamefacedly, Adam looked at the ground, and who knows, perhaps God smiled. Poor little man; so weak, so faulty, and yet so loved. Then God gave to him his first present—a coat of skins. Fear, incredulity, wonder, followed in quick succession as man lifted his eyes. "For me, O God? but what must I do for it?" "Nothing. Take it and put it on. This is the gift of grace through sacrifice. An offering has been slain to provide the garments of salvation." Ah, silly child, you cannot destroy divine love. God loves because He cannot stop loving. He is love. Accept God's gift, and be at peace. Then, as you journey through life, remember that although your sin may be great, the love of God is greater.

Adam, how wonderful is your God. He's mine, too.

NOAH . . . and his ship-load of strange guests

(GENESIS 6:20)

Until recent times higher criticism poured scorn upon this ancient account, dismissing it as one of the many Jewish legends said to be contained in the Old Testament. Bible dictionaries glibly spoke of " Noah's chest," and emphatically claimed it would have capsized had it ever been placed on the sea. These theories were made to appear foolish by the amazing discoveries of the archæologists. Sir Charles Marston's great book, " The Bible is true," tells the thrilling story of the uncovering of a great belt of clay. The brilliant men in charge of the excavations gave adequate consideration to the new findings, and were driven to the conclusion that there had been a deluge of vast proportions, and that the story of Noah's ark was not as silly as had been claimed. All who accept the Bible as the Word of God will gratefully acknowledge the corroboration of the archæologists; but even were this not available they would still believe the Scriptures, and consider Christ's acceptance of the account sufficient authority for their action. See Matthew 24:37-39.

The Strange Worry

If we could have stood on the slopes of an antediluvian hill, we would have witnessed a strange restlessness among the herds of animals grazing there. The beasts, hitherto content with their grazing lands, had suddenly become discontented. Within their breasts a strange urge suggested a move. Daily this increased, and finally, leaving the rest of the family, the disturbed beasts responded to the inward promptings and slowly walked away into the unknown. Thus God commenced the operation destined to maintain life in the new world. The critical commentators who scoffed at the idea of Noah's being commanded to collect the animals surely overlooked the statement, " Two of every sort *shall come unto thee,* to keep them alive." Noah was never expected to search for the animals. He had only to finish the work given to him. The Lord Jesus said, " As it was . . . so shall it be." The Spirit of God will be sent into all the world to move upon the hearts of responsive men. He will lead them to Christ, for in the world that

3

is yet to be will be representatives of " every people, and tongue, and nation " (Rev. 5:9).

The Strange Wisdom

How interesting it would be had we been able to understand the thoughts of the various animals as they obediently made their way toward Noah. Was the lowly rabbit of the field surprised to see the long-necked giraffe? Were the timid mice amazed as they saw the great lions slowly stalking toward the huge ship? Had some strange intuition enabled them to know that in this supreme matter of life and death, their safety depended not upon their strength or merit, for both the mighty and the weak were in equal danger? Apparently even the tallest animal realized that his only hope of survival lay within the ark. The greatest creature outside the ark would be in grave danger; the most timid one inside would be perfectly safe. Each animal had individually to avail itself of God's great provision. The Lord Jesus said, " As it was . . . so shall it be." God is determined to people His new world with the redeemed of all races, and to make this possible He perfected for us the ark of salvation. Man is not saved by works, neither is he helped by any sense of his own achievements. In response to the Holy Spirit's guidance, he must seek his safety in Christ.

The Strange Waiting

United in the common bond of brotherhood, the animals lost their fear of each other, and together entered within the shelter of Noah's ark. The human passengers followed, and the door was shut. All was now in readiness for the fulfilment of the preacher's message. Maybe the surging crowd of sightseers laughed loud and long when the expected storm failed to arrive. During the following week they wondered how long it would be before Noah reappeared. " And it came to pass *after seven days,* that the waters of the flood were upon the earth " (Gen. 7:10). Why did God wait a week before He sent the deluge? The answer is summed up in one word—*grace.* Alas, there were no seekers with sufficient faith to avail themselves of the new opportunity to ask admission. They were very near to safety, yet they were lost. And the Lord Jesus said, " As it was . . . so shall it be."

ABRAM ... the seeker who twice found God

(GENESIS 13:1-4)

There was trouble in Abram's home, and still more in his heart. His relatives were worried, and his friends were a little anxious. Abram, with a mystic look in his eyes, talked about a call, and declared that God had urged him to leave his father's country. His eyes sought the distant horizons. And from that day to this, man has questioned the cause of this sudden upheaval. Much has been said about Abram's father, but there is no mention of his mother. Had she died, and had Abram, stricken by grief, realized the futility of seeking comfort from idols? Was it in circumstances such as these that God called him? We are told in Acts 7:2 that the God of glory appeared unto him; but no details are given to explain how that appearance was made. Yet one thing remains indisputable: it is that, while Abram abode in Ur of the Chaldees, God spoke to him, calling him to a new country.

A Sinner Seeking for God

Imagination could paint a pretty picture of the difficulties facing this disturbed man. He contemplated leaving everything in order to embark upon an errand fraught with great danger. He had heard a voice, but could this have been the figment of fancy? Would the venture lead to disaster? These and probably many other thoughts flooded his mind, yet over all was the calm assurance that he had heard the voice of God. So he went on his journeys, until he came eventually to the place where he knelt at a little altar, and there to his amazement and joy " the Lord appeared unto him." Suddenly faith gave place to sight; the unknown, the distant, the inscrutable, became wondrously near and real. And is not this the experience of every Christian? John Bunyan has immortally enshrined this truth in the account of his famous character, Pilgrim. While the man abode in the city of Destruction, he could only hear the voice of Evangelist warning him to flee. When in response to the warning, Pilgrim came first to the slough of despond and ultimately to the Cross, his chains fell off, and in ecstasies of joy he discovered the reality of God. We may hear God anywhere, but we find Him at the altar.

A Saint Slipping from God

Abram's heavenly experience lasted just as long as he stayed near his altar. Bethel, the house of God, the place of fellowship, provided joys completely unknown in his former surroundings. Here he walked and talked with his God, and the entire earth seemed a paradise. Then for some unknown reason he made a mistake. "And Abram journeyed, going on still toward the south." The wanderlust had taken possession of his heart, and without divine direction he moved away from the place of blessing. This was a tragic mistake, for each step took him closer to Egypt. The next sentence in the story hardly needs comment—"And there was a famine in the land." Then Abram made his second mistake: he went down into Egypt.

Ah, stupid man, why did you not stay close to God's altar? You set a bad example for your many children. There is fellowship and sustenance in the presence of God; yet how many backsliders have slowly moved away toward Egypt's borders. The order seems to be a yard to-day, a few more to-morrow, and then suddenly we become conscious of a famine within the soul, and Egypt's corn becomes more desirable than ever before.

A Sinner Seeking for God Again

The account of Abram's experience in his far country makes sorry reading. He had no contact with God, and every day increased his misery. Faith was submerged by scheming, and peace replaced by anxiety. He almost lost his life. Then came the resurrection of his true self, for from the grave of disappointed hopes arose a new resolve to seek afresh the Author and Finisher of his faith. "And Abram went up out of Egypt . . . unto the place of the altar, which he had made there at the first." Once again he knelt on the sacred spot, and grace banished the shadows from his soul. Surely this ancient picture was painted by an Artist whose fingers bore the marks of omniscience. He who saw the end from the beginning, embodied His knowledge in the earliest of His writings. In His own way He was saying

There's a way back to God from the dark paths of sin;
There's a door that stands open and all may go in:
At Calvary's cross is where you begin,
    When you come as a sinner to Jesus.

6

LOT . . . who had to run for it

(GENESIS 19:16-22)

Dear Lot,

Were you ever really happy in Sodom? We have read the account of your parting from your uncle Abraham; we have followed you in thought to the cities of the plains; yet somehow you always seem to us to have been a misfit among the new surroundings and among the new people. We have read how you vexed your righteous soul, and were not at all surprised. The atmosphere of a stuffy city was no substitute for the clear air of the hills of God; and the people of Sodom were base in comparison with your saintly uncle. Do you remember that evening when you sat in the gate watching the approach of the two strangers? Do you recall with a start, the fear that chilled your heart when you contemplated the reception they would get from the depraved citizens? You did a noble thing when you took the travellers into your home. Well done, Lot. Many men would have been less courageous. Yes, we have been thinking about your story, and one or two things seem to be outstanding.

The Justice of God . . . Your danger was very great

There were obviously two types of people in your city. You represented a most noble kind, and yet in the nearby homes were men whose actions were extremely vile. It puzzles us how you ever managed to live among them. Your soul, Lot, surely shuddered at the very thought of their nearness. It is understandable why the prosperous plains attracted you. You were young, and had yet to learn that happiness is far more important than wealth. But, Lot, we have been staggered by the thought that although morally you were vastly superior to the Sodomites, your danger was equally as great as theirs while you stayed in their city. Human virtues count little when their possessor decides to remain in the place of condemnation. Yet such people live in our day. Villains and gentlemen live side by side in our world, and sometimes it is very difficult to persuade the latter that their goodness will be unavailing while they stay within the orbit of evil. Another thing puzzles us—

7

The Patience of God ... Your hesitancy was very strange

We listened eagerly, as it were, when the angel urged you to leave your city of destruction; we appreciated the great resolve that came to your soul, and were able to understand the chilling response of your sons-in-law. They probably thought you had taken leave of your senses, and immediately began the work of upsetting your plans to obey the command of God. You hesitated, and " he who hesitates is lost." Faith and doubt fought for the mastery of your heart; angel hands and family hands pulled in opposite directions, and your soul seemed torn asunder. And while this went on, God waited for you. Yes, He was very patient, and but for the fact that He has also been patient with us, we might be tempted to say that you never deserved such favour. Perhaps you realized the hurried departure would necessitate the abandonment of all your flocks and herds. Your decision would be most costly, for the savings of years would vanish overnight. Poor Lot, we sympathize with you; but my! weren't you fortunate that the angels took hold of your arm and refused to let go?

The Mercy of God ... Your escape was very wonderful

Yes, it was a near thing. You had to run for it! You were so reluctant to leave your earthly possessions, that your actions held up God's timetable of events. You were like many of us; in thinking of earthly loss you forgot to count the cost if your soul should be lost. It was a near thing for you, Lot; and to be honest, many of us feel you did not deserve God's kindness. We do not wish to offend you, Lot, but somehow, you seem to be like us—a little shallow. You did not like Sodom, but you were very partial to its sheep and cattle. We'll let you into a secret. We believed that somewhere would be an adequate reason for the miracle of your escape, and thus we patiently searched the old record for information. What do you think we found? We discovered in Genesis 19:29 a thrilling text. " And it came to pass, when God destroyed the cities of the plain, that God remembered Abraham, and sent Lot out of the midst of the overthrow." Brother, you were very fortunate. You had someone to pray for you— and God answers prayer.

ISAAC . . . who didn't let dirt get into his eyes
(Genesis 26:18)

" And Isaac digged again the wells of water, which they had digged in the days of Abraham his father; for the Philistines had stopped them after the death of Abraham. . . ." Isaac was a wise man. We should congratulate him. Dirt can be a great hindrance, especially when it spoils our vision.

A Great Drought

The need for water was urgent, and everyone realized it had to be found at all costs. Each passing day brought disaster nearer. The lowing of the cattle, the bleating of the sheep, and the lines of anxiety on the faces of worried men, told their own poignant tale. In a land where water was at a premium, the inhabitants valued it above gold. Isaac, the leader of the people, appreciated the urgency of the moment and faced his greatest problem. His anxious eyes searched the countryside where the drought had wasted the land and where the earth was bare and barren. He sighed as he watched his people, and his silent prayer went up to heaven. Oh, for a stream of living water!

A Great Decision

Isaac stood in the doorway of his tent, and resolution was born in his soul. He remembered how his father had passed this way, and how he also had been confronted by a similar need. He had found water. Isaac searched for those old wells, and frowned when he saw they had been filled with earth. The enemy had been busy. Obviously the springs had dried up, for no sane man would ever ruin a valuable well. To the followers of Isaac it seemed that Abraham's wells were no longer of use. Perhaps they would have passed by in their search for new springs; but Isaac stood still. The wells seemed to be utterly useless, and yet—his father had found water there. Could it be that beneath the rubbish the old springs were waiting to come to life? Would he be wise in looking beyond the dirt? He made his decision, and commanded his men to dig.

A Great Discovery

"And Isaac's servants digged in the valley, and found there a well of springing water." Other men would have considered the dirt and abandoned the task as hopeless. Rubbish would have impaired their vision. Isaac was too wise to permit the dirt to get into his eyes, and subsequent events proved the greatness of his decision. The toilers removed the rubbish from Abraham's wells, and soon a great cry of relief went up from the camp. The bubbling, sparkling flow of life-giving water arose to fill the well, and the desperation of anxious men gave place to praise. They had proved that the springs were still there.

A Great Declaration

Indeed, this is so important that it should be broadcast throughout the world. The need of man is still great. The fear of war, the unrest of human hearts, the intense yearning for reality can be found everywhere. It might be well to ask where our fathers found the sufficiency for their needs. They found that God was a refuge and strength, a very present help in time of trouble. The Church and the Bible were the wells in which they found refreshment. Yet to-day the man of the world scorns such ideas. He glibly declares that the Church is filled with rubbish and hypocrites. Alas, he has allowed dirt to get into his eyes. Nothing can alter the fact that millions of souls have proved that the old springs of God are still operative. If we have the determination to look beyond our disappointments we shall discover the springs of pardon, and peace, and eternal joy, are still realities, and our barren hearts will blossom as the rose.

"And he shewed me a pure river of water of life, clear as crystal, proceeding out of the throne of God and of the Lamb." There is no drought here! If I must dig, it is better to dig a well for my soul than a grave for my hopes.

ESAU ... whose stomach ran away with his brain

(GENESIS 25:29-34)

It is difficult for the people of western nations to appreciate the story of Esau's birthright, for many do not understand the importance attached by all peoples of the East to this inherent right of the first-born. We treat all children as equals, but the people of Bible lands regard the first-born son as the privileged one whose leadership must be undisputed, and whose inheritance will be twice as great as that of any other child. He has " the double portion " by right of birth. And in the light of Bible teaching the spiritual interpretation of this fact has become perfectly clear. By right of birth into the family of God, the Christian can lay claim to his birthright—a double portion of God's Spirit. Even Elisha realized the importance of this blessing, and earnestly asked his master to give to him " a double portion " of his spirit. The Christian birthright is not limited to select people, for God's bounty is infinitely greater than man's. Thus Peter was able to say, " For the promise is unto you, and to your children, and to all that are afar off, even as many as the Lord our God shall call " (Acts 2:39).

The Privilege of Power

" And Esau came from the field, and he was faint: And Esau said to Jacob, Feed me I pray thee ... Behold I am at the point to die, and what profit shall this birthright do to me? ... thus Esau despised his birthright." He ignored the fact that the traditional custom represented all that was sacred in their family life. The birthright included supreme honour and power in every matter related to the home, and was such that even Jacob became envious of his brother's privilege. That Jacob schemed to trap Esau cannot excuse the lustful brother whose only thought consisted of pleasing himself. In order to appease and satisfy the base longings of his inner life, he would have been content to sacrifice anything. It mattered not to him that his action would violate family laws, disappoint and break his aged father's heart, and bring dishonour upon the household. Self reigned unchallenged upon the throne of his evil desires, and he revealed clearly his unfitness to be anything other than what he was—a wild man of the fields!

The Price of Pottage

Probably Jacob realized his brother's weakness for pottage, and planned skilfully to tempt Esau into the sale of his birthright. When Esau requested a meal, Jacob replied, "Sell me this day thy birthright. And Esau replied, Behold I am at the point to die; and what profit shall this birthright do to me . . . and he sold his birthright to Jacob." His appetite robbed him of wisdom; his stomach ran away with his brain. His was the most expensive meal ever served, and it took him a lifetime to pay the account. Instead of reigning as a prince in the locality, he went about as an embittered beggar. Haunted by memories of his folly, and angered by his brother's magnificence, he became a man whose passionate moods robbed him of respect. The world has many examples of similar folly. David once cried, "Take not Thy holy Spirit from me," and even Paul visualized the possibility of becoming a castaway from the place of authority and power in God's service. No one can be filled with the power of the Holy Spirit if he permits the baser things of the flesh to rule his soul. The old man with all its affections and lusts must be crucified before resurrection life can fill and thrill the soul. Pottage was always an expensive item on the world's menu.

The Pain of Poverty

Centuries later, the writer to the Hebrews in speaking of Esau, "who for one morsel of meat sold his birthright," said, "For ye know that afterward, when he would have inherited the blessing, he was rejected: for he found no place of repentance, though he sought it carefully with tears" (Heb. 12:16, 17; Gen. 27:38). Esau was a man incapable of seeing fault in himself—and he was not the last to suffer from this strange disease of the eyes. We must learn from his sad story that, while repentance may bring pardon for sin, it cannot restore the lost opportunities of a bygone day. In the hour of temptation, self-denial may lead to eternal glory; surrender to base desires may lead to eternal sorrow. Some items of food are too expensive to buy. Our pockets, our health, our future may be seriously affected if we develop a liking for red pottage!

JACOB . . . who was hurt in a wrestling match

(Genesis 32:24, 25)

"And Jacob was left alone; and there wrestled a man with him until the breaking of the day. And when he saw that he prevailed not against him, he touched the hollow of his thigh; and the hollow of Jacob's thigh was out of joint, as he wrestled with him." Thus ended a series of battles that had been fought at varying intervals through many years. Jacob was a great fighter, and had never been defeated. Admittedly he was not too fussy about the methods used to obtain the verdict, and at times he should have been disqualified for dishonourable conduct. Yet always favour smiled upon him, and although on occasion one or two opponents had taken a couple of rounds in the struggle, the contests invariably ended in another victory for the relentless prodigal. And then at the height of his career, when he seemed an unbeaten champion at his art, an angel issued an annoying challenge.

The Contest Revealing a Great Determination

Jacob had always been a swindler and a cheat, and had never hesitated to take advantage of another man's weakness. Constantly he had matched his wits against opponents of all types, and had conquered. After many years in a foreign land he set his face toward his homeland, and planned by a series of magnificent gifts to offset the force of his brother's anger. Again he relied entirely upon his powers of scheming. His long procession of splendid presents was arranged to obtain the maximum effect upon Esau; but when the last of his family and friends had departed on the way to meet the oncoming brother, Jacob was left alone. And in the stillness of the night, the great challenge was presented personally. God's angel drew near to seize the great wrestler, and the conflict of the two antagonists beggared description. Horribly alone, Jacob refused to be beaten, and grappled with the unknown. Age was against him, but the struggle continued as Jacob grimly tried to outwit his opponent. Jacob was a grand fighter, and it seems a pity that his talents were always devoted to his own selfish ends.

The Collapse Revealing a Great Desire

We shall never know how Jacob discovered the identity of his opponent, for in the ferocity of that conflict, darkness had probably hidden both faces. Yet somehow Jacob sensed that he was wrestling against a superman, and then came the realization that God had come to challenge his powers of self-reliance. When he suddenly felt pain in his thigh joints, he knew his proud record of invincibility had gone. Desperately he seized the victor, and refused to loosen his hold. Suddenly a voice spoke from the darkness, " Let me go, for the day breaketh. And he said, I will not let thee go, except thou bless me." Tenaciously he clung to his Lord, and realized that even defeat would be turned to victory if the blessing of God fell upon his vanquished soul. It was then that Jacob was taught to pray. When the divine Trainer afterward attended to the injury, He decided to leave the thigh out of joint, and in compensation presented Jacob with a new heart. It was the best consolation prize ever given!

The Confidence Revealing a Great Deliverance

The voice said, " Thy name shall be called no more Jacob, but Israel: for as a prince hast thou power with God and with men, and hast prevailed. . . . And he blessed him there. And Jacob called the name of the place Peniel: for I have seen God face to face and my life is preserved. And as he passed over Penuel . . . the sun rose upon him, and he halted upon his thigh." The new day began with a reminder of his own weakness; yet he probably smiled—he was a prince with God! Permanent injury had enforced a premature retirement from the ring of carnal aggression; yet Jacob won more through his solitary defeat than he had won through his lifetime of unending conquests. He had discovered the secret place of the Most High, and had pitched his tent in the shadow of the Almighty. Realizing that he could never fight again, he became content to let God fight on his behalf. Wise fellow! Wrestling can be a very strange game—especially when one wrestles with God.

JOSEPH . . . in whose life God wrote a story
(GENESIS 37-41)

The types and shadows of the Old Testament are among the most thrilling of all Biblical studies. It is believed that holy men of old spake as they were moved by the Holy Spirit. In like manner it is believed that similar prophecies were produced in actions when men were led to do certain things in their daily life. It is for the reader to decide whether or not this may be accepted as fact, but Joseph's likeness to Christ is too striking to be accidental.

He was the Beloved of the Father (Gen. 37:3)

This was so displayed that it gave rise to jealousy. When he was presented with his coat of many colours, seeds of bitterness were sown in the hearts of his brothers.

He was sent on a Love Mission to his Brethren
(Gen. 37:13)

" And Israel said unto Joseph, Do not thy brethren feed the flock in Shechem? come, and I will send thee unto them. And he said unto him, Here am I." Thus the beloved of the father came seeking his absent brethren. Yet when he came unto his own, his own received him not. They conspired against him, and planned his death.

He was Sold for Pieces of Silver (Gen. 37:28)

It is surely not without interest that the sale was suggested by Judah. We think of Judas, who acted similarly with Christ. Thus Joseph was handed over to the Gentiles —in this case, the Midianite merchantmen.

He was Tempted . . . As we are, yet without sin
(Gen. 39:7-12)

The story of Potiphar's wife and of the treachery leading to Joseph's imprisonment needs no repetition. Amid the villainy of a foreign court Joseph maintained the purity of his soul, and so demonstrated his fitness for the great work entrusted to his care.

He Suffered for the Sins of Others (Gen. 39:20)

In his hour of darkness he was found with two notable

prisoners. To the one he spoke words of life; to the other words of death. We so easily remember Another who in parallel circumstances spoke words of hope to a repentant thief, while the second prisoner died in his sin.

Man placed Joseph in Prison, but the King brought him out
(Gen. 41:14)

After two years Pharaoh dreamed, and thus came the opportunity for the butler to speak concerning Joseph. "Then Pharaoh sent and called Joseph, and they brought him hastily out of the dungeon: and he shaved himself, and changed his raiment, and came in unto Pharaoh." Soon Joseph was exalted to the right hand of the king, where most effectively he could intercede on behalf of all who trusted him. Even so God raised up Jesus to be our Prince and Saviour. Now He ever liveth to make intercession for us.

Joseph foretold the Coming of Great Tribulation
(Gen. 41:29, 30)

He urged that certain preparations be made against the coming of the evil day, and his message proved to be a most effective way of salvation. Yet perhaps the greatest detail of all is that during the days of trial his own brethren after the flesh came to kneel before him. Those who had rejected and despised him now hailed him as saviour. And in similar fashion Christ spoke of the coming tribulation, when a fountain for sin and uncleanness will be opened to the inhabitants of Jerusalem. Israel will yet recognize their true Messiah.

Joseph had a Gentile Bride (Gen. 41:45)

"And Pharaoh called Joseph's name Zaphnath-paa-neah; and he gave him to wife Asenath the daughter of Poti-pherah priest of On. And Joseph went out over all the land of Egypt." Oh joy! the greatest part of the Bible story has yet to be fulfilled. The tragic rejection of Christ has been over-ruled for good. The Gospel has been preached among the Gentiles, and representatives of all people and kindreds and tongues will be at the marriage of the Lamb.

It was easy for Joseph to understudy Christ in this universal drama. The divine Author had written the script on his heart.

BALAAM . . . who couldn't make up his mind

" And the children of Israel set forward, and pitched in the plains of Moab on this side Jordan by Jericho. . . . And Moab was sore afraid of the people . . . and was distressed because of the children of Israel. . . . And Balak the king of the Moabites sent messengers unto Balaam saying. . . . Come now, therefore, I pray thee, curse me this people. . . . And the elders of Moab departed with the rewards of divination in their hands." And thus a most attractive temptation arrived to trouble the hesitant prophet.

PROPOSITION 1. *A sense of God's presence is no guarantee of His favour.*

Balaam listened to the request of the Moabites, and immediately sought the guidance of God. Alas, the Lord forbade his going with the elders of Moab. When greater nobles with increased rewards returned to tempt him, he again prayed for guidance and was told that if the request were repeated the following morning, he could accompany his visitors. Rising early, he saddled his ass, and ignoring God's condition he was ready to begin the journey even before the people who were to accompany him. Is it not therefore apparent that although he had received answers to his prayers, this was not evidence that he enjoyed the favour of the Lord? An intellectual apprehension of the truths of God can never be a substitute for a heart filled with His grace.

PROPOSITION 2. *A man's words are not always an indication of the integrity of his heart.*

Before Balaam reached the end of his journey a triple alliance had failed to arrest his progress. His conscience, his ass, and the angel had all stood in the way of his evil project, but the attracting power of gold had proved to be too great to resist. The prophet was led to a mountain from which he could see the camp of Israel spread out in the sunshine. A sense of security and calm emanated from those simple homes, and as Balaam considered the task for which he had been called, he hesitated—these people belonged to Jehovah. Suddenly he cried, " How shall I curse, whom God hath not cursed? . . . Who can count the dust of Jacob, and the number of the fourth part of Israel? Let me die the death of the righteous, and let my last end be like his!" (Num. 23:8, 10). Like John Bunyan's Mr. Talkative, Balaam's words indicated virtue of the highest quality, but were not a true indication of the state of his soul.

PROPOSITION 3. *A man's material possessions are not an indication of his true wealth.*

Balaam looked at the far-reaching camp, and probably sighed. The Israelites were so poor; they had nothing but the promises of God. He turned and looked at the kings who had so earnestly requested his help. They were so wealthy; they possessed everything but the promises of God. Oh dear! What should he do? He desired allegiance with both camps, but a choice was being forced upon him, and he could not make up his mind which to choose. Probably his old donkey would have been more decisive in the hour of crisis. There are things which money can never purchase. True riches are assessed by one's proximity to God; by one's faith in His promises, and by the peace received therefrom. God never leaves his people without a promise, and the promises of God are sure.

PROPOSITION 4. *A man's end is not always what he most fervently desired.*

A disappointed man, Balaam returned to his home. He had said too much to obtain eternal wealth; he had not said enough to obtain earthly riches. And later, when the armies of Israel swept through the land, he was overtaken and slain (Josh. 13:22). How easy it is to see him alone at his house. His mind is a prey to fear, his soul is the home of remorse, and his future is dark with gloom. Retribution is soon to overwhelm him, for he has delayed his decision so long that the time of opportunity has now passed for ever. His reputation as a prophet, his character as a man, and his hope for eternity were all ruined together. Centuries later, the apostle Peter spoke of the madness of the prophet Balaam. Such madness blurred his vision, emptied his pockets, and spoiled his life. To all people of this type the Scriptures say, " Choose ye this day whom ye will serve."

MOSES . . . and the Undertaker who buried him

(DEUTERONOMY 34:5, 6)

" So Moses the servant of the Lord died there in the land of Moab, according to the word of the Lord. And God buried him in a valley in the land of Moab, over against Beth-peor : but no man knoweth of his sepulchre unto this day." Thus ended the pilgrimage of one of the noblest of prophets. Moses, the friend of God, had been buried by his Friend. It was a great funeral!

A Revelation of God's Tenderness

Very slowly Moses climbed the hill, to be the central figure in the most solemn event of his career. Perhaps he paused at the turn of the road to look back at his beloved followers, and then resolutely he climbed to keep his appointment with God. We do not know what thoughts flooded his mind in those last moments, but according to a Jewish proverb, when he was ready " God took away his soul with a kiss." Then the Lord lifted His dear friend, and in the everlasting arms Moses was carried to the prepared grave. Relatives and friends were conspicuously absent; only the Undertaker was present. It seems a wonderful thing that He who created the worlds should covet the honour of performing the last rites over that still body. God must have greatly loved His servant.

A Revelation of God's Carefulness

" No man knoweth of his sepulchre unto this day." The children of Israel were very fickle in their choice of deities, and had they known the location of that hallowed spot, they might have made it a national shrine. Even Satan tried to alter the plans of God (Jude 9) and had he succeeded, the people would have fallen into idolatry. Omniscience prevented the sorrow that thus would have overtaken the race. God moves in a mysterious way His wonders to perform. He is too wise to err, and too loving ever to be unkind.

A Revelation of God's Holiness

Possibly Moses was grieved at the decision that forbade his entering the land. One sin prevented the attaining of his greatest joy; yet other people who had often sinned were permitted to reach Canaan. It seemed unfair. But God could not deal with the leader as He dealt with ordinary people. Moses was the great figurehead to whom all the people looked for guidance, and alas, he had failed. Each time afterward when he urged them calmly to do the will of God, their thoughts instinctively strayed back to the unfortunate incident in the wilderness. Had Moses been permitted to escape the consequences of his rash act, it would have seemed licence for the sinning of others. The entire nation knew cf the punishment following the failure of the great leader, and remembered that God was holy.

A Revelation of God's Thoughtfulness

When God terminated the ministry of Moses, He increased the effectiveness of his teaching. During the following years the memory of the great statesman provided the best incentive to faithfulness. S. D. Gordon suggests that each time a Hebrew mother told a bed-time story to her children, the experiences of Moses supplied the theme. And the children would listen intently as she spoke of the prince who had sacrificed all to become their leader. Their little eyes grew big with wonder as always the story ended in disappointment. " Children, he disobeyed God and was not permitted to enter the land. What a shame!"

Thus Israel was taught the lesson of obedience. It might be said of Moses as one said of Samson, that he accomplished more by his death than he ever did in life. Perhaps he knew this, and went home with a smile. And God buried him in some quiet corner where the flowers could bow in graceful salute, and where the birds could sing over his grave.

Isn't it marvellous how the presence of God can alter the entire atmosphere at a funeral!

JOSHUA . . . the man who took second place

(JOSHUA 5:13-15)

" And it came to pass, when Joshua was by Jericho, that he lifted up his eyes and looked, and, behold, there stood a man over against him with his sword drawn in his hand: and Joshua went unto him, and said unto him, Art thou for us, or for our adversaries? And he said, Nay; but as captain of the host of the Lord am I now come." These verses indicate a crucial point in the experiences of the children of Israel. When Moses had been taken away, the leadership had been undertaken by his servant Joshua, and thus Israel had crossed the Jordan and had successfully entered the promised land. The Lord had constantly watched over His people, but now an outstanding event took place. The young leader who had been second-in-command to Moses, continued in that rôle when the Lord descended to take charge of the nation.

The Lord would be Unfailing in His Presence

Joshua interviewed the mysterious Stranger, and discovered His illustrious identity. From that moment he knew God was near. Although the Lord did not again reveal Himself in the same way, Joshua realized He was close at hand, and this supplied constant encouragement as the time passed by. The promised land was a land of hills and valleys where experiences would vary from day to day, and yet never would Joshua be expected to carry his burdens alone. He was sure of God's nearness, and in quiet times of meditation could emulate the example of his predecessor and gain strength from communion with God. When first he saw the Stranger he drew near and questioned Him; but realizing that the Lord had come, he " fell on his face to the earth, and did worship, and said unto him, What saith my lord unto his servant?" Joshua's humility was most commendable, and clearly indicated his suitability for high office. The man who knows how to bow reverently before the Lord will be most suitable to occupy the important places in the councils of God's people.

The Lord would be Unfailing in His Power

" And, behold, there stood a man over against him

with his sword drawn in his hand." Joshua realized that the conquest of Canaan would not be an easy task. The cities had formidable defences, and the man-power of their armies was very great. Yet as he looked at the drawn sword of the Lord, he knew that " if God were for him, no man could be against him." In every time of crisis and emergency the Lord would fight on behalf of His people. The walls of Jericho would not be insurmountable barriers, if God went before the nation. Joshua rejoiced because he had been superseded in leadership, for he preferred to be second-in-command of God's army than first-in-command of his own. Many of the leaders who followed in after years had less wisdom, for they preferred to be chief of a remote village than second in an empire. They did not appreciate the fact that humility had power to exalt a man above kings. Joshua did, and falling upon his face to the ground, he worshipped, and asked for his Captain's orders.

The Lord would be Unfailing in His Purpose

" And the captain of the Lord's host said unto Joshua, Loose thy shoe from off thy foot; for the place whereon thou standest is holy. And Joshua did so." Humility led to reverence, and reverence to obedience; and Joshua was never a greater leader than when he was low at Christ's feet. There he revealed the true characteristics of statesmanship, for if a man knows how to maintain his place before God he will have no difficulties in maintaining his authority in the counsels of men. Within a few moments the vision had departed, and Joshua was left alone with his memories. Then, strengthened with spiritual might, he arose to assume command of the army. As the days passed by, he engaged the enemy and triumphed; yet in the cool of the evening he kept rendezvous with his Chief, to report on the operations of the day. The Book of Joshua describes the history of the Canaan campaign, and through all the varying vicissitudes of the conflicts, Joshua and his unseen Leader were in close collaboration, and thus ultimate victory was achieved. The purposes of God were fulfilled, and Israel entered into rest. It is a great honour to occupy second place, but only the best people qualify for the position. The Captain of our salvation is still with us, and we shall be safe if we abide in His shadow.

OTHNIEL . . . who won a bride in a battle

(JUDGES 1:12, 13)

Paul's greatest ambition was *to win Christ*. He wrote, "Yea doubtless, and I count all things but loss for the excellency of the knowledge of Christ Jesus my Lord: for whom I have suffered the loss of all things, and do count them but dung, *that I may win Christ*" (Phil. 3:8). Although he already knew Christ as his Saviour, he recognized there were greater heights of experience and deeper depths of intimacy still to be enjoyed. This is more easily appreciated in the light of an Old Testament story.

Love Concerned

The scene is set in Canaan, where old father Caleb faces his greatest task. Forty years earlier he had shared with Joshua the honour of bearing faithful witness to Israel, and as a reward had been promised for an inheritance the land over which his feet had trod. Now the nation has entered into the country, and Caleb has been told to "go up and possess it." But it was more easily said than done. Kirjath-sepher, an enemy stronghold, occupied a most strategic position in the coveted territory, and the old warrior realized the strength of its defences. He therefore issued a proclamation: "He that smiteth Kirjath-sepher and taketh it, to him will I give Achsah my daughter to wife." Probably he was thinking of his young nephew, already in love with his daughter. We do not know whether or not the boy had asked for her hand in matrimony, but if he had, the prize had been withheld, and Othniel was left with his all-important question—How can I win my beloved? The family link already existing, assured him of a welcome at all times; but he yearned to make her his very own. How like the great apostle is this boy of an earlier age! Paul also rejoiced in the union already existing between his Lord and himself, but he longed to know Christ more intimately, and for that joy counted all things but loss.

Love Challenged

"*He that taketh Kirjath-sepher.*" This was the greatest

challenge ever to reach the young warrior, and when its full implications burst upon his soul, resolution was instantly born. It mattered not how great the conflict might be; he scorned the dangers ahead, preferring to die in the enemy city than to live alone. Love answered the challenge in such a way that the historian was able to write, " And Othniel the son of Kenaz, Caleb's younger brother, took it: and he gave him Achsah his daughter to wife." There is no limit to what a man will attempt when love reigns within. This was the secret of Paul's indomitable courage. He had surveyed the country of his own soul, he had examined all the strong points of the inherent enemy, and with fierce determination to bring all things into subjection to Christ, he went forth to die daily. Often wounded and weary, often persecuted beyond measure, he had the glorious satisfaction of sharing with his Beloved a lifetime of fellowship. Such joys await all who take a dislike to Kirjath-sepher.

Love Conquering

" And it came to pass, when she came to him, that she moved him to ask of her father a field . . . then she said unto Caleb, Give me a blessing: for thou hast given me a south land; give me also springs of water. And Caleb gave her the upper springs and the nether springs." Artful lady, what would your father have said had he known of your plan? She smiles and coyly looks at her man. She possessed both beauty and brains—a rare combination! Her initiative and her husband's courage led to great things. He became one of Israel's greatest generals (Judges 3:9, 10). Thus God teaches us that in winning Christ we win everything. There is fabulous treasure in Kirjath-sepher, even though the road to the city be under enemy fire.

> Arise, ye men of God,
> And put your armour on:
> Strong in the strength that God supplies
> Through His eternal Son.

SAMSON ... and the price he paid for a haircut

(JUDGES 16:17)

And Samson said, "If I be shaven, then my strength will go from me, and I shall become weak, *and be like any other man."* Samson was not an ordinary man. His abnormal strength placed him in a category entirely his own. Rugged, fearless, invincible, he delivered Israel from the bondage of the Philistines, and under his leadership the people of God regained their independence. Yet the real secret of his strength lay not in his long hair but in his consecration. All through his life he had faithfully observed the vows made at his birth. He had remained a Nazarite, and this accounted for his power. His hair had remained uncut merely because this detail had been part of his promise. The cutting of his hair would indicate that he had ceased observing the laws of God, and this would mean sin. Against the sombre background of Philistine bondage we recognize in this inspired man the true hope of Israel. When brave people were beginning to lose courage, Samson came on the scene and revived all the latent longings of their hearts. He was God's man!

The Man Possessed

In comparison with others of his generation, Samson was a giant in spiritual stature. He stood alone. And it is not without interest that a man of this calibre has always been to the forefront whenever a religious awakening has come to the world. Sometimes he has been a product of the universities, but more often he has been an ordinary workman transformed by the power of God. True consecration lifted him above the realm of the ordinary, and in God's hand he became an instrument to overthrow the arrogant defiance of the authorities. Through such leaders as Luther and Wesley and others, conditions of true godliness unseen for many years have been restored to the Church. The great leaders followed Samson's example—they were unlike ordinary men. Spiritual strength elevated them to positions of supreme honour, and by observing their vows of consecration they gained for themselves the highest distinctions in the Kingdom of God. Yet every day they maintained an attitude of careful watchfulness, realizing that no degree of eloquence could ever compensate for the loss of spiritual power.

The Man Obsessed

The pitiable story of Samson's associations with Delilah provides one of the most disappointing accounts in history. Hindered by his own susceptibility to the enchantments of an attractive woman, his sickness of heart spread to his head. He believed he could outwit the wily daughter of his enemies, but became pliable clay in her capable hands. Her charms bewitched him; her roguery intrigued him; and as a moth finds it impossible to resist the attractiveness of the flame, so Samson lingered around the centre of feminine danger, and ultimately paid the price of his folly. The Philistines cut his hair, and the operation proved to be the most costly haircut in the history of mankind. He had no one to blame but himself, for on three occasions he had been furnished with sufficient evidence to prove the treachery of his sweetheart. He had played with sin, and the consequences had become fatal.

The Man Distressed

A ghastly sight, Samson stood in his prison and was hurt more by his memories than by his wounds. His merciless enemies laughed at the eyeless sockets—the two depressions of anguish in his agonized face. " They bound him with fetters of brass; and he did grind in the prison house." When Samson wearily sank to the floor at the end of the torturous labours of the day, no man could have been more miserable. " Howbeit the hair of his head began to grow again after he was shaven." And Samson allowed it to grow! He had fiercely resolved never again to break his vow. His former failure should remain alone in its isolation for ever. It seems an awful shame that the hot iron of the Philistine torturer did more for Samson than all the instruction given at Shiloh. A man is never so weak as when he is proud of his strength, and never so near to omnipotence as when in supreme weakness he clings to the promises of God. When Samson's brethren came to lift his body from among the shattered masonry of Dagon's temple, they probably realized that he had died happily. Yet a saintly man at the head of Israel would have been far more useful to God than a dignified corpse in a coffin. Samson's story should be a warning to every Christian leader throughout the world.

NAOMI . . . who left home and went back again

There are four scenes described in the Book of Ruth, and together they supply a most suggestive sequence of thought. They provide etchings the light and shade of which are superb.

Evening

Long ago, as the sun set in Israel, a man stood in his doorway looking over the barren countryside. It was harvest time, and there was no harvest! His face was lined, and perhaps a little cynical, for prolonged drought had ruined his crops. Barren fields, dying cattle, and sorrowful homes told of the dread famine which had overtaken the land. His silent wife knew of the bitterness of his soul, and stood listening with her two sons, when he said, " What is the use of staying here? The place belies its name. Bethlehem—the House of Bread—has become a place of famine. It should be called ' Ichabod,' for the glory has departed. It may be God's land, but I am going to leave it." And as the shadows gathered in his heart, the momentous decision was made. He would seek sustenance among the heathen in a foreign land. Alas, it was to be his most expensive journey! The ancient scene seems strangely modern. The Church has also been called the House of Bread, but sometimes the harvest fields have not been very fruitful. The place famous for its " Bread of Life " has often been a scene of disappointment. The road to Moab has been filled with people who turned their backs upon the fields of Bethlehem.

Night

Ten years later Naomi, dressed in the deepest mourning, sat in her Moabite home, and not far away three sombre mounds of earth silently witnessed to the sorrow which had devastated her soul. Her husband and the two boys had died, and she had been left with two daughters-in-law. Wearily she passed her hand over her eyes and remembered the nightmare experiences. At first they had prospered beyond their wildest dreams, and the little family felt able to support the two maidens with whom the boys had fallen in love. Then trouble mercilessly shattered their happiness. She had been presented with three Moabite graves. When people called her Naomi, she whispered, Sh! call me not Naomi, but Mara, for the Almighty hath dealt bitterly with me. Poor Naomi! Could she really expect to be happy while she was away from her homeland? And why blame God for her troubles when without His guidance she had wandered far from His house? Moab has a great reputation for graves.

Dawn

The dusty road ran through the countryside toward the Moabite border, and then on toward Bethlehem, where once again the fields echoed with the songs of the harvesters. Naomi had said "good-bye" to Orpah, but Ruth had refused to leave her. "So they two went until they came to Bethlehem." And the road to Bethlehem proved to be the road to God. Naomi, silent in her memories, sadly watched the harvest scene; Ruth, expectant with hope, eagerly scanned the new surroundings. The next morning, Ruth went out to glean in the fields of a kinsman. The wealthy Boaz secretly commanded the young men to help the strange maiden, and that evening, Ruth proudly displayed to her mother-in-law the abundance of her day's gleanings. When Naomi heard of the girl's adventures, she marvelled and instantly recognized that all things were working together for her good. The darkness of her soul's night was suddenly tinged with silver, and she saw signs of a new sunrise. Bethlehem is a marvellous place to see a sunrise!

Day

This scene should be divided into two sections, for in the top half should be the shadowy scene in the granary where the wealthy Boaz suddenly awakened from sleep to see the lovely Ruth at his feet. The account of that romance has thrilled mankind and demonstrated the fact that virtue is the greatest quality in the world. Twelve months later Naomi proudly looked at her beloved Ruth, and fondly nursed the child that had come to enrich the lives of Boaz and his Moabite bride. She remembered the troublous times of the past, and rejoiced in her new happiness.

HANNAH . . . whose investments brought great wealth

Someone has said, " Affliction is the Good Shepherd's black dog," and the truth underlying this epigram is particularly evident in the story of Hannah. She had a threefold cause for bitterness of soul. (i) " And her adversary also provoked her sore, for to make her fret." Peninnah's nagging was a grievous trial. (ii) "And it came to pass, as she continued praying before the Lord, that Eli marked her mouth." The priest thought she was drunk, and his harsh words might have had grave consequences. (iii) " The Lord had shut up her womb." Such was the belief current in those days, and had Hannah been bitter against God, her attitude would at least have been understandable. The disappointment of childlessness had impoverished her life, but nothing had spoiled the sanctity of her soul.

A Great Problem

God's problem far exceeded that of His handmaiden. Nagged by her household companion, and grieved by her chiidlessness, Hannah sorrowed daily; yet greater things were at stake in the purposes of God. He saw a nation slipping into sin, and had no instrument to use in the great work of rescuing His people. Hannah waited for a son, but God waited for a woman—a woman who would be willing to surrender her boy to God. While Hannah prayed, " O God, please give me a son," the Lord patiently listened to her cry and did nothing. When Hannah said, " O God, please give me a son, and I will give him unto the Lord all the days of his life," God realized that His waiting time had ended. God's delays always result in benedictions. He who sees the end from the beginning knows how to make " all things work together for good to those who are the called according to His purpose." God's time is always the best time.

A Great Prayer

" And Hannah vowed a vow, and said, O Lord of hosts, if thou wilt indeed look on the affliction of thine handmaid, and remember me, and not forget thine handmaid, but will give unto thine handmaid a man child, then I will give him unto the Lord all the days of his life, and there shall no razor come upon his head. . . . Now Hannah spake in her heart; only her lips moved, but her voice was not heard. Therefore Eli thought she had been drunken " (1 Sam. 1:11-13). True prayer cannot always be recognized by the excellent phraseology in which the petitions are expressed. A falling tear may be far more eloquent than grammar, and a sigh far more effective than the most lengthy intercession. Hannah possessed an intense faith in God, and in spite of repeated setbacks, continued to make known her requirements. Refusing to be ensnared into the carnality of quarrelling with her temptress, she maintained her purity of soul, and her prayers reached the heart of God. " Then Eli answered and said, Go in peace; and the God of Israel grant thee thy petition that thou hast asked of Him."

A Great Provision

" Wherefore it came to pass . . . after Hannah had conceived, that she bare a son, and called his name Samuel." God always honours His promises, but sometimes He does so in superb ways. The delay occasioned in Hannah's life resulted in unbelievable blessing, for not only did Hannah receive her boy, but God found an instrument of blessing, and Israel found a saviour. The sacrifice made by the brave and faithful woman was destined to obtain an abiding place among the outstanding acts of the elect. Had she fondled and retained her boy at home, Israel would have perished, and in the overthrow perhaps even Samuel would have died. She dedicated him to the service of God, and left him in the care of the aged priest at Shiloh. She invested her newly acquired wealth in the bank of heaven, and within a few years gained interest far in excess of anything she had ever considered possible. " And the Lord visited Hannah, so that she conceived, and bare three sons and two daughters. And the child Samuel grew before the Lord " (1 Sam. 2:21). The loneliness of her heart was banished for ever by the child-laughter which rang continuously through the house. " And the child Samuel grew on, and was in favour both with the Lord, and also with men." Her investment brought great wealth, for heaven's bank always pays outstanding dividends!

NABAL . . . the wealthy pauper

If birth certificates were issued in ancient times, the registrar had a great shock when he wrote the new baby's name—Nabal. He would have stared and then asked, " But why give such a silly name to the child? It means ' fool,' and the lad will be the laughing-stock of all people." Yet the parents for some unexplained reason remained adamant, and the new arrival began life with a name destined to be prophetical. Had it been the custom to erect tombstones over graves, and to inscribe a true record of the person there buried, the sculptor responsible for Nabal's grave would have written, " His name was true. He was a great fool." Every act in the strange life of this wealthy farmer betrayed folly of unprecedented dimensions. His foolish temper robbed him of his servants' respect; his foolish drunkenness cost him his wife's love; his foolish selfishness deprived him of a guardian's care; and his folly in sinning ruined his soul.

Grace Watching

It was shearing time at Nabal's farm, and the bleating of the many sheep herded together in the sheepfolds echoed over the countryside. Nabal, the wealthy farmer, stood watching his perspiring slaves, and his foul temper was often evident in his dealings with the toilers. He wanted the maximum amount of work done for the least possible pay, and his brutal methods made one of the workmen say, " He is such a son of Belial, that a man cannot speak to him." When David's men arrived to seek food in return for their untiring care of the flocks in the wilderness, Nabal raved and drove them away hungry. He ignored the fact that God's servant had refrained from taking supplies, and revealed that gratitude was unknown in his heart. He was a wealthy pauper who possessed nothing but money, and in the final analysis, he did not possess that; it possessed him.

Grace Working

Unknown to the ignorant man, retribution was swiftly descending upon his head as his loyal wife went forth to intercept the avenger. David's anger had been aroused, and he was hurrying to the scene of the insult when Abigail, Nabal's wife, fell at his feet. His heart was strangely stirred when she cried, " Upon me, my lord, upon me let this iniquity be." The sincere intercession of that great woman protected her sinful husband, for David refrained from carrying out his plans of vengeance. Had Abigail sought selfish interests she would have allowed David to exact his vengeance, but resisting any inclinations toward that end she interceded for her man, and succeeded beyond her wildest dreams. Nabal should have thanked God for the faithfulness of a good wife. And so should many other men, for he was not the last to profit through the prayers of a devoted woman. Alas, the foolish farmer was too short-sighted to recognize that, contrary to all he deserved, the grace of God still worked on his behalf.

Grace Waiting

" And Abigail came to Nabal; and, behold, he held a feast in his house, like the feast of a king; and Nabal's heart was merry within him, for he was very drunken." Wisely she refrained from telling him of the events of the evening, but when " the wine was gone out of Nabal, and his wife had told him all these things, that his heart died within him, and he became as a stone." Either the fact that he had lost some of his possessions, or that his wife had acted without his authority, aroused his resentment to such a degree that, in modern parlance, he had a stroke. Yet he was not finally smitten until another ten days had passed. During this respite he lay in his embittered helplessness, probably bemoaning the fate that had interfered with his freedom of movement. Perhaps he did not know how to pray, for he had been a long time without practice. At last even God admitted the uselessness of further delay, and the soul of a fool was taken into the eternal shadows. Grace could not wait for ever. In the closing moments of Nabal's life all his former actions seemed futile and irresponsible. He had lived for self, and had lived completely in vain. His money provided everything for an elaborate funeral, but it could not purchase a place in heaven. Eternal poverty provided a sad contrast to earthly luxury—and, alas, he had a very long time in which to study the difference.

THE NAMELESS SLAVE . . . who made a name for himself

"So David and his men came to the city, and, behold, it was burned with fire; and their wives, and their sons, and their daughters were taken captive. Then David and the people that were with him lifted up their voice and wept, until they had no more power to weep" (v. 4). All around lay the ruins of their devastated city. A foul enemy had raided the place during the absence of the men, and every home had been destroyed by fire. The blackened timbers, the swirling clouds of smoke, and the awful silence broken only by the crackling of flames, told their own poignant story. Somewhere beyond the horizon the triumphant enemy had driven the womenfolk into a captivity worse than death, and when the despairing men considered the untold horrors that would be employed to break the dauntless spirits of Israel's womanhood, "they wept until they had no more power to weep." "And David inquired at the Lord, saying, Shall I pursue after this troop? shall I overtake them? And He answered him, Pursue: for thou shalt surely overtake them, and without fail recover all. . . . And they found an Egyptian in the field."

How Serious His Situation

"And David said unto him, To whom belongest thou? and whence art thou? And he said, I am a young man of Egypt, servant to an Amalekite; and my master left me, because three days agone I fell sick. . . . We made an invasion . . . and burned Ziklag with fire." The plight of that unfortunate slave had been most critical. Deserted by his slave owner, he had been left to perish in the merciless heat of an eastern sun. Friendless and forsaken, he had lain for days without food and water, and had lost all hope of survival. Yet as he discovered the identity of the man who stood over him, his terror increased. He had helped to burn this stranger's home, and had assisted in driving his family into unspeakable bondage. He deserved death, and if the Israelite captain decided to take the law into his own hands, there would be no court of appeal against his sentence. The dying Egyptian quickly realized that even death would be preferable to torture, and the outraged feelings of these distracted men would be capable of anything—even torture.

How Surprising His Salvation

"And David said unto him, Canst thou bring me down to this company?" And as the young man looked up into the eyes of his questioner, he realized that in spite of the enormity of his crime, there was still a chance to escape execution. He looked at the listening men who had allowed the life-giving water to trickle down his parched throat, and their kindly smiles reassured him. This was neither dream nor trickery, for David was willing to offer mercy. It seemed too good to be true; but then he realized this was not an unconditional offer of mercy. David's grace must be equalled by his own responsibility. Salvation would only be possible if he were willing to change masters. David required his services, and he had therefore to renounce the old task-master and seek rest in the service of a new lord. "And he said, Swear unto me by God, that thou wilt neither kill me, nor deliver me into the hands of my master, and I will bring thee down to this company." When he regained his strength and was able to stand, he knew he had received a pardon he had not deserved.

How Splendid His Service

He therefore determined to prove to his new master the extent of his gratitude. His best talents should be devoted to the cause of David, and the rescue of the other unfortunate men and women whose bondage would be as cruel as his own had been. "And when he had brought David down, behold, the Amalekites were spread abroad on the earth, eating and drinking and dancing. . . . And David smote them from the twilight even until the evening of the next day. . . . And David recovered all." Probably the young helper watched the emancipation of the slaves, and rejoiced in the part he had been able to play in making their release possible. He had faithfully served the man who had graciously saved him from death. And thus once again the divine Author enshrined in an ancient story the triple truths of the Saviour, salvation, and service. Our debt to Christ is very great. We must therefore heed the words of Paul, and "present our bodies a living sacrifice . . . which is our reasonable service."

THE MEN OF JABESH GI
never forgot

It was night, and the flicker
disturbed the stillness of Israel'
around, but none desired convers
be alone with their memories, even the
were bitter. They would remember for ever the
experience when they had fled from a scene of no...
Their king was dead, their homes occupied by heathens,
their loved ones dead or—they shuddered as they thought
of other possibilities. Their future outlook was as bleak
as the winds of winter, for it would be but a matter of time
before these hateful conquerors, drunk with success and
lusting for further conquests, would press forward into the
country. And since the might of Israel had fallen, nothing
remained to prevent the complete subjugation of the land.
Moodily they stared into the fire, and all around the night
was mysterious and still. Suddenly, unannounced and
unexpected, diversion came to perform a miracle in the
hearts of despondent men.

We are not informed as to the identity of the messenger,
and imagination alone seems able to supply the necessary
details. A man staggered out of the eerie darkness, and as
he approached the fire, watching men hurried to his
assistance. Perhaps some of them recognized him and
unthinkingly blurted out their questions, " Where have you
been? How did you escape in the battle? We had given
you up as dead." Slowly he shook his weary head and told
of his escape from Bethshan. He told of the mockery of
their pagan conquerors; he told of the decapitation of Saul.
There could be no mistake, for he had seen these terrors.
He had been there. He sighed, and in the moments that
followed a remarkable thing took place. Men approached
from the shadows, and at the sound of their voices the
newcomer looked up. His tale was told again.

The men stood awhile considering, and finally their
leader spoke. His voice was more like the growl of an
angered beast. It was low, and quiet, and deadly. His
eyes seemed to throw back the challenge of the firelight,
and when he moved, his actions were those of a man who
knew exactly what he intended to do. " Men, we are going

an." Immediately the others signified their
l, and to the bewilderment of the listening
tes, within minutes they had commenced their
ney. In recording those illustrious moments, the
torian wrote: " And when the inhabitants of Jabesh-
gilead heard of that which the Philistines had done to Saul;
all the valiant men arose, and went all night, and took the
body of Saul, and the bodies of his sons, from the wall of
Bethshan, and came to Jabesh, and burnt them there. And
they took their bones and buried them under a tree at
Jabesh, and fasted seven days." We can only ask why
these men risked their lives in such an enterprise.

The answer is supplied in the earlier history of the city.
Years before, an Ammonite invasion had taken place, and
Jabesh-gilead had been surrounded by merciless enemies.
The heathen king Nahash, with conspicuous conceit, sat in
his royal tent and waited. His captains were in command
of the situation; his lines were unbroken. Jabesh-gilead
would fall. He was satisfied. When emissaries sought
peace terms, he replied: " On this condition will I make a
covenant with you, that I may thrust out all your right eyes,
and lay it for a reproach on Israel. And the elders of Israel
said, Give us seven days' respite, that we may send
messengers unto all the coasts of Israel; and then, if there
be no man to save us, we will come out to thee " (1 Sam.
11:1-3). Nahash indulgently agreed. He knew the
messengers would need to pass through his camp. He
would be waiting for them. Yes, the respite was granted.
Yet in spite of all his watchfulness, one young man at least
penetrated the heathen lines and carried the news far into
Israel. Saul the son of Kish heard of the plight of his
brethren, "And the Spirit of the Lord came upon him."
He led his army to the battle, and the men of Jabesh were
saved. They never forgot their saviour. They loved him,
and could never rest while his body was being made an
object of scorn. Their exploit is one of the most
courageous recorded in history. Three shining words stand
out in their record—gratitude, gallantry, glory. They did
this for their dead saviour. What would we do for the
living Christ?

ABNER . . . whose pride paralysed his feet

(2 SAMUEL 3:27)

If David had been invited to write the inscription for Abner's tombstone, his first attempt would probably have been something like this—" In affectionate memory of a great man who threw away his life." And in that one tragic statement would lie one of the saddest of Old Testament stories. Poor Abner was a great fool.

How Serious His Danger

The battle was almost over, and with the bitterness of defeat beginning to overwhelm him, Abner ordered his men to retreat. The forces of David, led by General Joab, had gained the ascendancy, and not wishing to sacrifice his men needlessly, Abner mercifully ordered them to flee. It was a case of every man for himself. As Abner ran through the countryside, he realized that he was being followed by Asahel, Joab's youngest brother, and unwilling to slay the young man he cried a warning. " Then Abner looked behind him, and said, Art thou Asahel? And he answered, I am. And Abner said to him, Turn thee aside to thy right hand or to thy left, and lay thee hold on one of the young men. . . . But Asahel would not. And Abner said again . . . Turn thee aside . . . wherefore should I smite thee to the ground? How then should I hold up my face to Joab thy brother? Howbeit Asahel refused " (2 Sam. 2:20-23). Abner killed the pursuing soldier; but from the moment Asahel fell, his slayer was in deadly danger. The law demanded " an eye for an eye, and a tooth for a tooth," and Abner realized that once Joab heard of this unfortunate occurrence, he would vow vengeance. Abner's one hope was to flee to a city of refuge. God had made ample provision for such emergencies, and Abner had only to present himself before the priest to find safety.

How Stupid His Delay

His face set in hard, grim lines. Wisdom urged obedience to the commands of God. Pride warned him that his flight would become known to all Israel. People might interpret this as an act of fear. Probably self-righteousness put up a praiseworthy argument. Why should he take the place of a guilty man? Had not his deed been committed in self-defence? Had he not warned the stupid boy whose impetuosity had overpowered his brain? No, Israel should never be given occasion to sneer. They should know he was not afraid of Joab or any other man. Proudly he followed his troops. Yet he was still in danger, for all his arguments would never alter the fact that Joab was entitled to his " eye for an eye." Abner was a silly man. He was a valiant warrior on every field of battle except the battlefield of his own soul.

How Sudden His Death

The scene has changed. Abner has offered his services to David, and the offer has been accepted. The magnificence of the royal reception has overwhelmed the old General, and he returns to persuade his troops to support David's cause. Joab has returned to camp, and has been told of Abner's visit. Hastily summoning young men, he sent them after his old enemy with commands to bring him back. Unwittingly Abner returned to Hebron, to find Joab waiting for him in the gateway. This was their first meeting since the death of Asahel, and as tension mounted Abner permitted himself to be led aside. Hebron was one of the cities of refuge, and since Abner was actually in the gateway, he was only a step from safety. Probably many onlookers were watching the proceedings, and any insistence on Joab coming into the city would betray nervous hesitance. Wisdom cried aloud for immediate action, but pride paralysed his feet. His folly robbed him of life. " Joab smote him there . . . for the blood of Asahel his brother."

How true to life is this ancient story. We are sinners also, but God has made provision for our safety. Within the city of Christ's eternal care, we can find security, Alas, many people who have heard and understood the Gospel fail to respond. They know what they should do, but they will not do it. Pride is a creeping paralysis. It begins in the heart and ends with the feet.

OBED-EDOM . . . whose parlour became a sanctuary

(2 SAMUEL 6:11)

" Obed-edom, I envy you a great deal. Not many people have the honour of a sanctuary in the parlour. Not every day does God go to live in a humble cottage. I would have liked to stand with you watching when King David came down into your district to take away the sacred ark of God. Were you excited when the thirty thousand fighting men paraded in the fields? Were you thrilled when the massed royal bands played on all manner of instruments; and did your heart nearly stop when they reverently carried the ark from the house of Abinadab? Were you shocked when the tragedy took place a few yards from your homestead?

The Man who Died

" I have been wondering a great deal about that event, for it seems so strange, Obed-edom, that God's hand of judgment should fall on a man apparently trying to do good. Oh yes, I know the people had broken the law. The sacred furniture should have been carried on the shoulders of the priests, and not bumped on a wagon; but still, why should Uzzah suffer for the sins of others? It is very strange, Obed-edom. I wonder what you thought. Now, I may be wrong, but I'll tell you what I think: that God hates hypocrisy. He is not pleased when men are two-faced. Obed-edom, did you ever hear of Ananias and Sapphira, and how they died because they were hypocrites? I have wondered if Uzzah were like them. Had he hated the ark, considering it to be a nuisance taking up valuable room in the small cottage? Then suddenly, when the king came, he posed as its proud custodian. I cannot be sure; but perhaps, Obed-edom, you could give me a better idea?

The Man who Doubted

" And poor King David! I think I am sorry for him, although he was a little stupid, don't you think? Of course, he had had a great shock, and his best plans were all wrecked, but surely he was silly to run off home like a spoilt schoolboy. I think it would have been wiser to try to discover the cause of the upset. There must have been some reason for it; but there, my brother, we humans are so queer. We always like to have things our way, and are so upset when God interferes with our plans. I can almost see the shadows on David's face, and hear his whispered mutterings of self-pity. Why are we so quick to believe the worst and slow to believe the best?

The Man who Decided

"In thought I have often stood with you, Obed-edom, to watch the disappearing crowds. I have often looked at the perplexed officer who stood alongside the new cart. I have tried to imagine what you said to him. Was it something like this?

"'Officer, what are you going to do now? If you agree, I shall be so pleased to have the ark in my parlour.' And was he amazed? Did he ask, 'Sir, are you not afraid?'· Did you reply, 'No one with a clean heart need fear God'? And so they carried it—Him—in. Of course, they gave you a breathing space in which to prepare, and then in a moment your parlour became a temple. Fortunate man, Obed-edom! But I'll let you into a secret, and I know you will be envious. You had the ark for three months, didn't you? I am more fortunate. He has come to live in my heart. One day I heard a voice saying, 'Behold, I stand at the door, and knock: if any man hear my voice, and open the door, I will come in to him, and will sup with him, and he with me.' When I opened the door, He came in. We have been together ever since. He's wonderful. Good-bye."

P.S.:

I tell Him all my sorrows,
I tell Him all my joys;
I tell Him all that pleases me,
I tell Him what annoys.
He tells me what I ought to do,
He shows me how to try;
And so we walk together,
My Lord and I.

SHIMEI . . . and the ghost that killed him

(2 SAMUEL 16:5-8; 1 KINGS 2:8, 9)

It has been said that a policeman can always be recognized by his feet! The same is true of a saint, for the Christian's walk is indicative of his character. Alas, many people are like Nebuchadnezzar's image—they have a head of gold and feet of clay. I sorrowfully confess that one of my Biblical idols has proved to be of this type. David, the sweet singer of Israel, ended his life in discord. He whose songs of praise had reached highest heaven, failed to hold his note, and the harmony of a lifetime was shattered.

A Guilty Man

Treachery in the city had forced David to flee. The incoming of Absalom and his evil associates had threatened murder, and David with a few of his faithful friends had slipped away into the country. Then suddenly a man came running across the fields. " And when king David came to Bahurim, behold, thence came out a man of the family of the house of Saul, whose name was Shimei, the son of Gera: he came forth, and cursed still as he came. And he cast stones at David . . . and said Come out . . . thou bloody man. . . . The Lord hath returned upon thee all the blood of the house of Saul. . . . Then said Abishai unto the king, Why should this dead dog curse my lord the king? let me go over, I pray thee, and take off his head. . . . And the king said, Let him curse." Thus a very guilty man was spared. He deserved death, but David forbade his execution.

A Gracious Monarch

The scene has changed. The deciding battle has been fought and won, and the king returns to his palace. " So the king returned . . . and Shimei came down with the men of Judah to meet king David. . . . But Abishai said, Shall not Shimei be put to death for this, because he cursed the Lord's anointed? And the king said unto Shimei, Thou shalt not die. And the king sware unto him " (2 Sam. 19:15-23). David's actions at this time have won the

41

admiration of a world. Shimei had great cause for gratitude. Forgiveness is a wonderful thing—when it is forgiveness. David seems a giant among virtuous men— but, alas, his feet were of clay! Thirty years later, " The days of David drew nigh that he should die; and he charged Solomon his son, saying, I go the way of all the earth: be thou strong, therefore, and shew thyself a man. . . . And, behold, thou hast with thee Shimei . . . who cursed me with a grievous curse. . . . Now therefore hold him not guiltless . . . his hoar head bring thou down to the grave with blood " (1 Kings 2:1-9). What a tragedy! Surely our sweet psalmist was out of tune!

A Ghastly Murder

This final request of King David is among the most disappointing things of history. Apparently he had forgiven the offender, but had retained his bitter memories. He had forgiven but had not forgotten Shimei's sin. The subsequent story of murder has been told for us in 1 Kings 2:36-46. Some may attach blame to Shimei for disobeying Solomon, but nothing will ever alter David's last request. Even Solomon seems to be condemned by the fact that the man whose execution he ordered had been one of the faithful during the insurrection of Adonijah (1 Kings 1:8). Those were days when personal loyalty and genuine gratitude were sacrificed on the altar of passion. How refreshing it is to turn to the words of God in Jeremiah 31:34, " I will forgive their iniquity, *and I will remember their sin no more.*" When God forgives, He forgets: herein lies our security and peace. The precious blood of Jesus washed our sins away for ever. The ghost of Shimei's past returned after thirty years. His arrival was inopportune and tragic. I'm so glad I met Christ. I don't believe in ghosts—now.

> Gone, Gone, Gone, Gone,
> Yes, my sins are gone:
> Now my soul is free,
> And in my heart's a song.
> Buried in the deepest sea,
> Yes, that's good enough for me:
> I shall live eternally;
> Praise God, my sins are gone.

MEPHIBOSHETH . . . and his glorious wretchedness (2 SAMUEL 19:24)

" And Mephibosheth the son of Saul came down to meet the king, and had neither dressed his feet, nor trimmed his beard, nor washed his clothes, from the day the king departed until the day he came again in peace." And this marked the highlight of David's homecoming. It is exceedingly interesting to know that this unlovely sight is perhaps the most charming picture seen in the experiences of King David. The story of Mephibosheth falls into two sections, and is best appreciated that way.

The Salvation of a Sinner

It was a poignant scene when the prince, Jonathan, revealed to David his knowledge of the identity of Israel's future king. God had chosen David, and by so doing had rejected the house of Saul. Jonathan, whose love for David surpassed the love of women, rejoiced in the favour shown to his friend, and one day asked David to remember him in the day of his ultimate triumph, and show kindness to his children. But many years had passed before David said, " Is there yet any that is left of the house of Saul, that I may shew him kindness for Jonathan's sake? . . . And Ziba said unto the king, Jonathan hath yet a son which is lame on his feet. . . . Then king David sent and fetched him out of the house of Machir, the son of Ammiel in Lodebar." It is so easy to visualize the coming of the royal servant to the house in the wilderness, and to understand the suspicion with which he was received. Mephibosheth belonged to the house of Saul, and expected hatred from David's line. But all his fears were subdued when the great offer of salvation was made known. He was made to understand that he could never merit this gift of David; he could never earn it; he did not deserve to receive it. This was a gift made entirely for Jonathan's sake. The crippled fellow could hardly believe his good fortune; but sweeping aside all his doubts, he gladly accepted the offered mercy and was lifted out of his wilderness home and brought to the palace. The Old Testament picture seems to have been painted with New Testament colours. God offers salvation to the sinner. Man can never deserve nor earn this treasure, and no works of righteousness can ever merit it. It is the supreme gift of the love of God, because One greatly beloved has died. "God for Christ's sake has forgiven you," said the apostle, and in every presentation of the Gospel message we have the fulfilment of the veiled foreshadowings enshrined in the story of the ancient cripple. Alas, many people seem to be less intelligent than he. They prefer a home in the wilderness.

The Faithfulness of a Saint

The scene has greatly changed, for rebellion has broken out in the city of Jerusalem. Fleeing from the murderous intentions of Absalom, David has escaped into the country-side, where he is met by Ziba the servant of Mephibosheth. "And the king said, And where is thy master's son? And Ziba said unto the king, Behold, he abideth at Jerusalem: for he said, To-day shall the house of Israel restore me the kingdom of my father. Then said the king to Ziba, Behold, thine are all that pertained to Mephibosheth" (2 Sam. 16:3, 4). Alas, the convert upon whom so much grace had been showered was now seen to be unreliable—or so it seemed. Later, when the battle for the kingdom had been won, David returned to find Mephibosheth awaiting his coming. The king asked, "Wherefore wentest thou not with me, Mephibosheth?" And in reply he heard of the treachery of Ziba. The servant had slandered his master in the hope of obtaining royal favour. We can almost hear Mephibosheth's whispered appeal, "Master, if you have any doubt, just look at me." And David's eyes grew strangely misty when he beheld the utter wretchedness of the cripple. His wounds had not been cleansed; the bandages remained unchanged; and his entire appearance suggested pain and neglect. Realizing that he had been slandered before his royal saviour, Mephibosheth per-sistently refused to flirt with the usurper prince and remained an object of scorn throughout Absalom's stay in the city.

This Old Testament scene wonderfully illustrates the whole theme of the Gospel. In this present day our Saviour is the despised and rejected One, for the prince of this world is attempting to steal the kingdom. Yet soon the ultimate triumph will be won, and He will return. Have we been loyal to Him during His absence?

ADONIJAH . . . from whose coronation party the guests ran away (1 KINGS 1:45-50)

Adonijah, the would-be king, was in great danger, and he knew it! Before him stood the tables of his coronation banquet, and all around the spacious chamber distinguished guests sat in their places of honour. The high priest and Joab, commander of the army, sat on either side of the throne, and many noblemen graced the gathering. Yet a grim silence had hushed the congratulatory speeches. Jonathan, the son of the high priest, had entered the hall to announce the latest news from the city. He told how King David had heard of Adonijah's plan to steal the kingdom, and had prevented it by commissioning the prophet Nathan immediately to crown Prince Solomon. A great congregation of Israel had already witnessed the ceremony, and had shouted "Long live the king." This announcement brought deadly fear to the gathering, and one after the other the guests hurried from the room. Finally, Adonijah was left alone.

The Man and His Problem

The guilty pretender to the throne considered his predicament, and made three startling discoveries. (i) He recognized that, according to the law of the land, he was a great sinner. He had known of David's intention concerning a successor to the throne, but had rebelled against the appointment of Solomon. His heart had cried, " I will not have this man to reign over me," and he had carefully laid his plans to assume kingship. He had failed in his attempt, and was obviously guilty of treason. (ii) He recognized that he was a sinner *in very great danger*. The law knew little of mercy, and as soon as Solomon became acquainted with the evil intentions of the usurper, he would begin the great man-hunt and continue it until Adonijah had been found and executed. (iii) He recognized that if he intended to seek safety, there was need to hurry. Soon all chance of escape would have gone. To linger complacently would reveal folly of the most serious kind. He had to do something, and do it quickly.

The Man and His Perception

What could he do? Where could he flee? He realized that although he took the wings of the morning to fly to the end of the earth, the long arm of his brother's vengeance would ultimately reach out and take him. If he sought a hiding place, his brother's servants would never rest until they had tracked him down. What then could he do? To remain inactive, hoping things would take a turn for the better, was out of the question. He knew his position was most critical, for he stood condemned as a traitor and fully deserved the fate about to overtake him. Then, as he desperately faced his problem, a possible way of escape opened up before him, and ruthlessly slaying any vestige of pride remaining in his heart, he "feared because of Solomon, and arose, and went, and caught hold on the horns of the altar." He knew his only chance of escape lay in taking hold on the place which testified of sacrifice and forgiveness. He ran quickly to the sanctuary, and climbing on the altar, he wrapped his arms around the place where the blood of the offering had been sprinkled, and then adamantly refused to descend.

The Man and His Pardon

"And it was told Solomon, saying, Behold Adonijah feareth king Solomon: for, lo, he hath caught hold on the horns of the altar. . . . And Solomon said, If he will shew himself a worthy man, there shall not an hair of him fall to the earth: but if wickedness shall be found in him, he shall die. . . . And he came and bowed himself to king Solomon." Thus a guilty man received his pardon. It is easy to discover in this ancient account another evidence of the inspiration of Scripture. Only God who is able to see the end of things from the beginning could ever express in history the Gospel message yet to be revealed. Old Testament altars were finger-posts pointing onward to the glorious fulfilment of all prophetic utterances. The Lord Jesus came to take away sin; and the work which the Father had given Him to do, He completed at the Cross. There alone can the guilty find pardon. If man has already discovered his threefold need, he has only to hasten to this place of supreme sacrifice, and in faith lay hold on God's altar. There the grace of God dispenses forgiveness; there the guilty find rest.

ELIJAH . . . whose drying brook led to a reservoir

Elijah belonged to Gilead, in the highlands of Israel, where—like their land—the people were rugged and unconquered. Forests lined the hilltops, and wild beasts roamed in the valleys. His simple garments of skins, his rippling muscles, his utter fearlessness, marked him as a true son of the people. He feared none but God. When news of Ahab's sin reached the upland villages, this strange man was greatly shocked; and it was not a cause for amazement when he wrapped his mantle around him and began his journey toward the royal palace. His fiery denunciation of the royal evils, and his threat of heaven's reprisal, were sufficient to bring about his death; but probably the noblemen were greatly amused by the primitive appearance of this foolhardy preacher, and permitted his escape. Obeying the commands of God, Elijah turned eastward and found a luxuriant valley in which to hide.

The Leafy Sanctuary—How safe is the guardianship of God

His temporary home seemed like nature's cathedral. The interlacing branches of the trees formed the roof of his sanctuary; the music of the brook which came tumbling from the hills sounded as though an invisible musician played on the great organ; and when the wind gently blew upon the leaves of the trees, it was easy to believe the seraphim had moved their wings. Every day, Elijah's feathered friends brought food; and as he drank of the brook, he knew God was very near. His valley was a haven of peace. The emissaries of the royal court were seeking the man whose prediction had come true, but in this delightful hiding place Elijah was perfectly safe. Only those people who have experienced the intimacies of such fellowship can appreciate this joy. There has never been any substitute for fellowship with God. When one lives in conscious communion with the Almighty, inward peace becomes a reality and fear is instantly banished. The man of God was always secure while he abode in the will of God. And so shall we be if we follow his example.

The Little Stream—How strange is the guidance of God

" And it came to pass after a while, that the brook dried up." Elijah awakened one morning to discover the music of his little stream was not quite as boisterous as it had been. He realized his friend was about to die; and when the disquieting silence descended on his valley, the shadows momentarily gathered on his face. His delightful holiday had ended. How much did Elijah know? Did he realize his enemies were already following the course of the stream in the vain hope of finding water? Did he know that within twenty-four hours his hallowed sanctuary would be invaded by wicked men who would not hesitate to kill him? God's ways are always wiser than ours. Before the stream finally ceased its murmurings, it seemed to whisper, " Child, it is time to move onward." Many people still linger alongside their drying brooks. Financial, domestic, friendship, and even health streams can all dry up, and the modern Elijah can easily become downcast— especially if he has poor eyesight!

The Listening Saint—How sublime is the grace of God

Elijah heard the voice of God saying, " Arise, get thee to Zarephath, which belongeth to Zidon, and dwell there : behold, I have commanded a widow woman there to sustain thee." The man of God obeyed, and by so doing he not only preserved his own life, but also became a means whereby God met the need of others. A widow woman " went and did according to the saying of Elijah : and she, and he, and her house, did eat many days. And the barrel of meal wasted not, neither did the cruse of oil fail, according to the word of the Lord, which He spake by Elijah (vv. 15, 16). During his time of sojourn in this simple home, the servant of God enjoyed fellowship with other trusting saints, and probably realized this was far better than living alone in the most charming of valleys. One's happiness can never be complete unless one is instrumental in increasing the happiness of other people. The drying of Elijah's brook set his feet on the path to a reservoir where supplies of living water were limitless. He had learned to camp alongside " a pure river of water of life, clear as crystal."

ELISHA . . . who never failed

(2 Kings 2:13, 14)

There was not a single instance of failure recorded in the ministry of the prophet Elisha. His record perfectly illustrates New Testament doctrines. Accompanying his master he had reached the Jordan, and had gone down into the river—the place of death. Together they arose, in type of resurrection, and journeyed toward the place from which Elijah ascended into heaven. After this Elijah's mantle, which had been the symbol of his power, returned to empower the waiting servant. We are reminded of the truth expressed in the sixth chapter of Romans. Positionally we were with Christ when He went to His cross. Paul declared, "Knowing this, that our old man is crucified with Christ." "We are buried with Him by baptism into death." God reckons this to have been accomplished for us in Christ. Yet the positional truth of identification with Christ must be translated into practical experience; and all this was wonderfully illustrated in the story of Elisha.

He was filled with the Holy Spirit

" And Elisha took hold of his own clothes, and rent them in two pieces. He took up also the mantle of Elijah that fell from him, and went back and stood by the bank of Jordan." ·Renouncing his self-life, he tore his own garments and deliberately walked where his master had trod—he went down into the river. This was the Old Testament way of saying, " I am crucified with Christ: nevertheless I live; and yet not I, but Christ liveth in me." In figure, he passed through death and rose triumphantly on the other side. Then daily he walked in the will of God, and failure was never known in his ministry. If we may liken him to the Church, his was the perfect type of the Spirit-filled life—he was like Christ.

He was Able to Raise the Dead

It is recorded of the Shunammite's son, " And he said unto his father, My head, my head. And he said to a lad, Carry him to his mother. And when he had taken him, and brought him to his mother, he sat on her knees till noon, and then died. And she went up, and laid him on the bed of the man of God. . . . Then she saddled an ass . . .

and came unto the man of God." The prophet responded to her appeal, and eventually restored her son to life (2 Kings 4:19-36; Luke 7:15).

He was Able to Feed the Hungry

"And there came a man from Baal-shalisha, and brought the man of God . . . twenty loaves of barley. . . . And Elisha said, Give unto the people, that they may eat. And his servitor said, What, should I set this before a hundred men? He said again, Give the people, that they may eat: for thus saith the Lord, *They shall eat and shall leave thereof.* So he set it before them, and they did eat, and left thereof, according to the word of the Lord (2 Kings 4:42-44; Matt. 16:9, 10).

He was Able to Cleanse Lepers

"And Elisha sent a messenger unto Naaman, saying, Go and wash in Jordan seven times, and thy flesh shall come again to thee, and thou shalt be clean. . . . Then went Naaman down, and dipped himself seven times in Jordan, according to the saying of the man of God: and his flesh came again like unto the flesh of a little child, and he was clean " (2 Kings 5:10-14; Matt. 8:1-3).

He was Able to Open the Eyes of the Blind

"And it came to pass, when the Syrians were come into Samaria, that Elisha said, Lord, open the eyes of these men, that they may see. And the Lord opened their eyes, and they saw; and, behold, they were in the midst of Samaria " (2 Kings 6:20; Luke 18:35-43).

Life was Given through his Death

"And Elisha died, and they buried him. And the . . . Moabites invaded the land. . . . And it came to pass, as they were burying a man, that, behold, they spied a band of men; and they cast the man into the sepulchre of Elisha: and when the man was let down, and touched the bones of Elisha, he revived, and stood up on his feet " (2 Kings 13:20, 21; John 3:16).

Elisha was filled with the power of the Holy Spirit, but this was not merely an experience of the past; it was rather the outworking of divine energy in every phase of his ministry. His Jordan experience enabled him to walk daily in " newness of life." He succeeded: and so shall we—*if we know how to die !*

NABOTH . . . the commoner who upset a king

(1 KINGS 21:3)

"Naboth the Jezreelite had a vineyard . . . hard by the palace of Ahab king of Samaria," and that charming place provided one of the most picturesque sights in Israel. The young owner constantly attended to its requirements, for it represented all that was best in his life. His father and his father's fathers had worked in this vineyard, and had finally bequeathed it to him, a most sacred possession. It was "the inheritance of his fathers," and according to the commands of Moses should never be sold.

A Suggestion Scorned

"And Ahab spake unto Naboth, saying, Give me thy vineyard, that I may have it for a garden of herbs . . . and I will give thee for it a better vineyard than it; or, if it seem good to thee, I will give thee the worth of it in money." And as the young man listened to his royal master, he realized that the hand of material prosperity was knocking on the door of his heart. The king was greatly attracted to the well-kept place, and offered great honours in exchange for it. The transaction would produce opportunities of increasing his personal wealth, and appeared to be a very good bargain. Yet, this vineyard was the inheritance of his fathers; and as he remembered that Scripture forbade the sale of such property, he realized that no amount of material gain could ever compensate for the loss of his paradise. "And Naboth said to Ahab, The Lord forbid it me, that I should give the inheritance of my fathers unto thee." This old story has a modern application. The inheritance of *our* fathers would be other than a vineyard. If we were to ask where lay the source of their joy, the answer would surely be most illuminating. The Church, the Lord's day, the Word of God, and their great love of eternal realities, seem to be the outstanding features of the inheritance handed down to us. Ahab reminds us of the glamorous *prince of this world* who seeks to entice us into parting from our place of seclusion and peace.

A Saint Stoned

" And Ahab came into his house heavy and displeased
. . . and he laid himself down upon his bed, and turned
away his face, and would eat no bread." Jezebel sought
an explanation of his sudden illness, and hearing of
Naboth's obstinacy, she undertook to break his resistance.
Aided by the religious leaders, she planned his betrayal,
and " they carried him forth out of the city, and stoned
him with stones, that he died." He had no regrets, for
he knew there were worse calamities than death. Had he
lived in dishonour, his burdens would have been intoler-
ably heavier to bear. As the stones rained upon him, he
found comfort in the thought that at least he would have
a clear conscience when he rejoined his fathers. He was
laying down his life in order that he might find it again
and keep it for ever. Yes, he was quite content. His
conscience was clear; his heart was at rest.

A Schemer Startled

" And Jezebel heard that Naboth was dead . . . and she
said unto Ahab, Arise, take possession of the vineyard of
Naboth the Jezreelite, which he refused to give thee for
money, for Naboth is not alive, but dead." And as she
smiled she seemed to add, " Now you get it for nothing."
But she was wrong. This was to be his most costly
purchase; he was to pay with his life. Excitedly he hurried
to his new possession, and came face to face with the
prophet Elijah. Startled and dismayed he cried, " Hast
thou found me, O mine enemy? And Elijah answered, I
have found thee: because *thou hast sold thyself.*"—" Thus
saith the Lord, In the place where dogs licked the blood of
Naboth shall dogs lick thy blood, even thine." In robbing
a saintly young man, Ahab had sold himself into the eternal
bondage of sin. Jezebel's ink had written his own
execution order; the well-laid plans had reacted as a
boomerang, and had returned to thwart the realization of
his fondest dreams. And although his repentance gained
a little respite, the end of his sad career was never in
doubt. In gaining a vineyard, Ahab lost his soul. Naboth
lost his vineyard, but preserved his honour. He was a
shrewd business man after all!

THE THREE CAPTAINS . . . who climbed a mountain to die

(2 KINGS 1:9-13)

The entire nation talked of the great accident. King Ahaziah had fallen through a lattice in his upper chamber, and had been seriously hurt. The news had spread rapidly, and many people feared that the consequences would be fatal. The monarch lay upon his bed tortured by superstitious fears, and his mental deterioration increased continually. Unable to bear the suspense, he summoned messengers and sent them to the priests of the god of Ekron, to seek information regarding the outcome of the unfortunate accident. Soon the messengers returned with the news that the prophet Elijah had met them and announced words of impending doom. The infuriated king immediately ordered the capture of this annoying servant of God; but by this time Elijah sat calmly on a high hill awaiting the retaliation of the evil ruler.

Captain Indifference

"Then the king sent unto him a captain of fifty with his fifty. And he went up . . . and spake unto him, Thou man of God, the king hath said, Come down." The scene on the hillside was filled with great drama, and the only man unconcerned was the captain whose career was about to terminate. The king's command was supreme, he thought; the prophet had no alternative than to obey! This was to the captain merely a routine job, and the sooner it was completed, the better for all concerned. "So, man of God, come down." His attitude probably reflected the attitude of the nation. The fear of God was a thing of the past; respect for His servants had disappeared. These decadent tendencies had to be arrested before final tragedy overtook the nation. The mountain scene was but a stage in the national theatre. The eyes of a countrywide audience would be watching the unfolding of the drama. "And Elijah answered . . . If I be a man of God, then let fire come down from heaven, and consume thee and thy fifty." It did, and Elijah grimly awaited their successors.

Captain Ignorance

"Again the king sent unto him another captain of fifty with his fifty. And he answered and said unto him, O

man of God, thus hath the king said, Come down quickly."
The additional word in the command acts as a small
window through which we are able to see the new captain.
He was resourceful and arrogant. He knew what he had to
do, and he intended to do it. He was not a man to be
defied. "Come down quickly—or—." He was very
different from his predecessor, and no one could accuse him
of indifference. He bristled with efficiency! He feared
neither God nor man. His order would be obeyed
immediately, or there would be great trouble for the dis-
obedient preacher. He seemed totally ignorant of God's
holiness, God's power, and God's law. He was certainly
ignorant of the spiritual strength of Elijah. Alas, he and
his men perished.

Captain Intelligence

When the news of the second tragedy reached the
barracks, fear placed its hand on every heart; and when
the stubborn king deliberately sent a third company in
search of the invincible prophet, the newly commissioned
captain realized that he approached the greatest crisis in
his life. "And the third captain of fifty went up, and
came and fell on his knees before Elijah, and besought
him, and said unto him, O man of God, I pray thee, let my
life, and the life of these fifty thy servants, be precious
in thy sight." His attitude suggested respect, reverence,
and the fear of God. His statement, "these fifty thy
servants," signified his recognition of the man of God as
the real master of the situation. The command of Elijah
carried greater authority than that of the king, and in any
final decision, the soldiers would prefer to be true to the
prophet rather than loyal to their supreme military
commander. The captain's prayer saved the life of every
soldier present, and taught that God is never inaccessible
to the man whose heart is contrite. *Law* painted this
ancient picture, but *grace* has supplied a New Testament
equivalent. A Pharisee and a publican went into the
temple to pray. The self-righteous citizen drew near to the
altar, and advertised his virtues; the publican stood afar
off, and reached the heart of God. Captain Intelligence
and the Publican appear to be twin souls. Their united
testimony will be most profitable for any who seek their
company.

THE FOUR LEPERS ... who became evange-
lists
(2 KINGS 7:10)

" There were four leprous men at the entering in of the gate," and their plight was desperate. The nearby city had become a place of dread, where famine and death stalked unchallenged through the streets, where cries of anguish were wrung from hearts of grief. The Syrians had surrounded the capital, and there was no chance of relief. Caught between the arrogant enemy and the stubborn defenders, the lepers were starving. Then a great resolve formed in their minds, and they decided to approach the enemy camp, saying, " If they save us alive, we shall live; and if they kill us, we shall but die." Thus they walked among the Syrian tents, and discovered that God had provided a great salvation for Israel.

How Sublime the Declaration

" Then they said one to another, We do not well: this day is a day of good tidings, and we hold our peace . . . now therefore come, that we may go and tell the king's household." And so it came to pass that the four lepers hurried to the city, and with every means at their disposal endeavoured to attract the attention of the men who kept the gate. Their message of God's free salvation seemed a fantasy, and the people inside the stricken city had difficulty in believing it. Yet the lepers persisted in their efforts, declaring that they also had been in doubt before despair had driven them to the Syrian camp. They were quite sure of the reality of what God had done, and could faithfully promise relief if only the starving inhabitants would come forth in search of food. Those lepers were indeed evangelists, and were really knocking upon people's hearts. The city so easily reminds us of men and women within whom is a famine for the bread of life. Inward misery and hopelessness have darkened their outlook, and they live in ignorance of the great work already accomplished on their behalf. God in Christ has provided salvation, and man has only to believe and respond in order to prove the reality of the Gospel. Every soul-winner follows in the footsteps of the four lepers of Israel.

How Senseless the Delay

When the king heard the great news, he " arose in the

night, and said unto his servants, I will now shew you what the Syrians have done to us. They know that we be hungry; therefore are they gone out of the camp to hide themselves in the field, saying, When they come out of the city, we shall catch them alive, and get into the city." The pessimism of the royal leader depressed the entire population, and sadly they wondered if the new message were a hoax. Their attitude was very foolish, for the message proclaimed by the lepers could easily have been proved. Then one of the servants suggested the sending of investigators. And the king said, " Go and see." Perhaps the most commendable feature about the Gospel of Christ is that in like manner its message may be examined. The Saviour invited all who were weary and heavy laden to come to Him for rest. No other leader has ever been able to make such a promise. The wealthy may offer money; the wise may offer advice; the experienced may promise guidance; but none can give rest except Christ. To remain hopelessly despondent within a city of gloom seems to be the height of folly when a way of escape has been provided.

How Simple the Discovery

When the servants of the king bravely went forth to meet the unknown, they quickly discovered that the lepers had been faithful messengers of great news. The Lord had indeed performed a miracle, bringing fear to the hearts of their enemies. "And they returned and told the king." Furiously they drove their chariot horses across the plains, and the watching people upon the walls of the city surely marvelled at the recklessness of their driving. The men dashed up to the gate, and as quickly as possible told their story. As the people listened to the thrilling testimony of their own friends, their doubts disappeared, and they rushed forth to avail themselves of God's bounty. Thus was the city of Samaria saved when hope had almost been abandoned. Let us remember that, although God provided the salvation for the people, He did not open the door of their city. See Revelation 3:20.

THE SHUNAMMITE . . . who proved God knows what He's doing (2 KINGS 4:8-37; 8:1-6)

"And it fell on a day, that Elisha passed to Shunem where was a great woman." This text admits of three possible interpretations. (i) She was great in physical stature; (ii) She was great in social importance; (iii) She was great in spiritual power. Eastern nations regard women with a certain amount of scorn; they consider them to be insignificant and unrequired except in the duties of a household. It is therefore of interest that the Shunammite was said to be a great woman.

She was Great in Her Kindness

It is easy to see the long, dusty road and the farmhouse lying back in the field. The sun shone from a cloudless sky while a woman dreamily looked over the countryside. Suddenly she saw two weary travellers coming along the road, and wondered why they were not resting. She extended a welcome to both Elisha and his servant, and they gratefully entered into her hospitable home. God graciously rewarded her kindness when He fulfilled all the innate longings of her soul and gave to her a son. When death prematurely claimed the boy, she successfully appealed to the servant of God, and the boy was restored to life. The story of that great event was destined to have far-reaching repercussions.

She was Great in Her Obedience

"Then spake Elisha unto the woman whose son he had restored to life, saying, Arise, and go thou and thine household, and sojourn wheresoever thou canst sojourn, for the Lord hath called for a famine; and it shall also come upon the land seven years. And the woman arose, and did after the saying of the man of God" (2 Kings 8:1, 2). It was not easy to leave all her possessions, for she had no guarantee that she would ever see them again. Other people would move into her empty home, and her lands would not be permitted to remain idle. Yet although her future path seemed fraught with great peril, she obeyed the saying of the man of God. "She went with her household, and sojourned in the land of the Philistines seven years."

We would like to ask her whether or not she ever worried about the things she had left behind, or did she rest in faith believing that He who had commenced a good work would be able to complete it?

She was Great in Her Reward

Her case appeared to be hopeless when after seven years she decided to return home to appeal to the king for her lands. The Bible story reminds us of a great chess board where a master hand patiently moves the pieces into position. First, let us consider that Elisha's servant had become a leper, and consequently had been banished from the intimate company of his fellow-men. He was " a leper as white as snow "—*but he could not die*. It was absolutely imperative that he be kept alive. Secondly, let us consider how the king suddenly became interested in the exploits of the prophet for whose ministry he had formerly had little interest. Absorbed with the desire to hear of miracles, he overcame his reluctance to be near a leper, and sent for Gehazi. Thirdly, we must remember there were many items from which to choose an acceptable story, but Gehazi spoke of the raising of the Shunammite's son. Fourthly, let us note how God so perfectly timed the woman's arrival. He knew exactly how long it would take to walk from the land of the Philistines, and had timed the king's interest and the leper's thoughts so that they dovetailed into each other. " And it came to pass, *as he was telling* the king how Elisha had restored a dead body to life, that, behold, the woman, whose son he had restored to life, cried to the king for her house and her lands. And Gehazi said, My lord, O king, this is the woman, and this is her son, whom Elisha restored to life. And when the king asked the woman, she told him. So the king appointed unto her a certain officer, saying, Restore all that was hers, and all the fruits of the field since the day that she left the land, even until now " (2 Kings 8 : 5, 6).

She smiled. Her God knew what He was doing, and she was perfectly safe in His care. She had been on holiday, and had not even been obliged to pay men to sow and harvest her crops. She had sought first the Kingdom of God and His righteousness, and in a most remarkable way, all other things had been added unto her.

JEHOIADA . . . who made a big money box

(2 KINGS 12:9)

This strange story begins with the account of how a brave princess rescued a little boy from certain death. "Athaliah arose and destroyed all the seed royal. But Jehosheba . . . took Joash the son of Ahaziah, and stole him from among the king's sons which were slain. . . . And he was with her hid in the house of the Lord six years" (2 Kings 11:1-3). During the whole of the period, Jehoiada the priest watched over the young prince. When Joash was allowed to leave his hiding place, he often saw the damaged places of the temple, and if he sought reasons for the dilapidation, the priest sorrowfully told him of the evil influences at work in the nation.

The Need for a Revival

When Joash became king, a new era began in the spiritual life of Israel. "He did that which was right in the sight of the Lord all his days wherein Jehoiada the priest instructed him." He remembered the damaged house of God, and recognized the great need for a revival of true godliness. The house of the Lord had lost its glory, and the entire nation had become decadent. The young king considered the spiritual poverty of the people, and formulated his plans. He said to the priests, "All the money of the dedicated things that is brought into the house of the Lord. . . Let the priests take it to them, every man of his acquaintance: and let them repair the breaches of the house, wheresoever any breach shall be found."

The Hindrances to a Revival

During the following years the king realized that the work was not progressing; he therefore called for Jehoiada and the other priests, and said unto them, "Why repair ye not the breaches of the house? Now therefore receive no more money of your acquaintance, but deliver it for the breaches of the house. And the priests consented to receive no more money of the people, neither to repair the breaches of the house." There are three possibilities in regard to the cause of this tragic delay. (i) The people were not bringing sufficient money to the priests, and thus the work was hindered. (ii) **The** priests were misappropriating God's money, and using it for themselves. (iii) The builders were not hurrying to complete the task. Revival could never come to Israel while there were so many hindrances within the temple itself.

The Signs of a Revival

The actions of the wise old priest revealed his genius. " He took a chest, and bored a hole in the lid of it, *and set it beside the altar* . . . and the priests that kept the door put therein all the money that was brought into the house of the Lord . . . and there was much money in the chest." Every man who approached the money box first saw the altar. He could hardly give without remembering the greatness of God's gift to him, and the strong probability is that the unusual position of the money box occasioned a great deal of thought, and resulted in the increase of the offerings. It is not possible for any man to give a true offering until he has first lingered near the Cross. It is possible to sing, " Take my silver and my gold," and then offer coppers to God. The old priest was exceedingly wise when he placed his money chest in such a thought-provoking position.

The Coming of Revival

" And they gave the money, being told, into the hands of them that did the work, that had the oversight of the house of the Lord : and they laid it out to the carpenters and builders. . . . And to masons, and hewers of stone, and to buy timber. . . . Moreover they reckoned not with the men, into whose hand they delivered the money to be bestowed on workmen: for they dealt faithfully." The carpenter stood at the money box and realized that his gift could never be as great as the altar demanded. He therefore decided to increase it with his consecrated service. The mason and all the other workmen had similar experiences, and finally added to their monetary contributions their faithful labours. In a very short time the breaches of the house were repaired, and the temple began to acquire its former grandeur. Revival had not only come to the sacred house; it had reached the hearts of the people. The vision of the altar had revolutionized the people's giving. It always does!

JEHOIACHIN ... who was in prison for thirty-seven years (2 KINGS 25:27-30)

The prison was dark and sombre, a place of gloom, where hope had long since died. Throughout the hours of daylight, merciless guards enforced the rigours of hard labour; and throughout the night, weary prisoners were alone with their memories. Jehoiachin, the one-time king of Judah, was a particularly sad case, for thirty-seven years of imprisonment had crushed his spirit. Year after year he had languished in his prison cell; youth had given place to middle age, and now he grew old before the time. There were occasions when he would have welcomed death, for nothing could be worse than the bondage experienced in a Babylonian dungeon.

A Great Prince

Unknown to the captive king, a young prince, whose attitude contrasted greatly with that of the prevailing royal house, had become favourably disposed toward him. Babylonian law knew no mercy until this prince manifestated grace. Secretly he had desired to liberate the famous prisoner, but this had been impossible. He therefore planned for the future, when supreme power would rest in his own hands. "And it came to pass in the seven and thirtieth year of the captivity of Jehoiachin ... that Evil-merodach king of Babylon *in the year that he began to reign* did lift up the head of Jehoiachin out of prison." Here were veiled foreshadowings of New Testament truth, and if it were possible to change the name of the Babylonian, many people would prefer to call him "Prince Grace."

A Great Pardon

When the captive was informed of the liberation order, he had difficulty in accepting its authenticity. It could not be true that his former enmity would now be forgotten, and his earlier resistance to the State pardoned. Yet it was true! In contrast to the previous régime, the new one offered kindness to the king of Judah. Jehoiachin had neither to earn nor merit his gracious pardon. It was offered as the free gift of the new monarch. He had only to accept the king's grace, and he would be free. In like manner, the Prince of peace delights in offering mercy. Frustration almost defeats His efforts while He is kept from the throne, but once He reaches the supreme place within the kingdom of the human heart, He offers pardon " without money and without price."

A Great Power

Jehoiachin's initial joy might have been somewhat spoiled by premonitions that he would find many enemies in the new life of freedom. All Babylonians were not of the type now offering mercy. Brutal overlords would endeavour to renew his misery and bondage. Perhaps he asked himself if he would be able to maintain what was then being offered, and it would not have taken long to realize his own great weakness. But then someone revealed the magnitude of the king's offer. " And he spake kindly to him, *and set his throne above the throne of the kings that were with him in Babylon."* The great prince who had offered mercy had also made ample provision to meet future requirements. If forces were liberated to enslave Jehoiachin, his power would be sufficient to offset the challenge. And so it is in the Christian faith. The Saviour not only offers pardon to the sinner; He gives power to the faint, and in those harassing moments when we cry, " O wretched man that I am! who shall deliver me?", we are able to continue, " I thank God through Jesus Christ."

A Great Provision

" And the king changed his prison garments: and he did eat bread continually before him all the days of his life." The two men lived and dined together, and each found in the other the fellowship for which his soul yearned. Thus did God set forth beforehand the mysteries of the salvation to be provided in Christ. " My God shall supply all your need according to His riches in glory by Christ Jesus " (Phil. 4:19). Jehoiachin would have been a very foolish man had he rejected the king's amazing offer; and " How shall we escape if we neglect so great salvation? " (Heb. 2:3).

ASA . . . the king with the bad feet

(2 CHRONICLES 16:12)

There is a way that leads to God, and all around it are three classes of people. Some are looking for the way, and cannot find it; some have found it, but refuse to walk along it; others have found it, and are walking heavenward. King Asa belonged to the second class. As a young man he had faced his greatest crisis when a vast host of heathen Ethiopians had invaded his country. His small army had been greatly outnumbered, but his desperate prayer had brought miraculous relief and at the same time had opened his own eyes to the nearness of God (2 Chron. 14:8-12). The discovery added greatly to his responsibilities. In the excitement of his triumph the young king made many vows; but in the years that followed, those vows were completely forgotten. His formation of a sinful alliance necessitated the visit of a prophet, and the final result was tragic. Enraged, King Asa ordered the imprisonment of God's messenger, and within a few days he himself was stricken by disease.

A Great Disease

"And Asa in the thirty-ninth year of his reign was diseased in his feet, until his disease was exceeding great." Undoubtedly the best physicians were called to diagnose and treat the complaint, and probably they promised ultimate recovery; but the fact remained that every day the disease increased its hold upon the suffering patient. Yet the greatest tragedy of all was that the trouble in his feet was but symptomatic of the illness of his soul. The petition of his sincere heart would have done more than the greatest physician. Every true instinct in Asa urged prayer, but even as he considered the project his face set in grim lines of determination. If this were to be a fight with a prophet and his God, it should be a fight to the finish. What a silly man! Pride is a foul monster with a beautiful face, and only those with vision can ruthlessly crush him.

A Great Mistake

"Yet in his disease he sought not to the Lord, but to his

physicians." At first I feel inclined to say, "Poor man," but on second thoughts I would add, "Poor physicians." The king expected them to do so much, and in the final analysis they could do nothing. Surgical skill is an amazing wonder, yet some of the greatest physicians readily admit the limitations of their art. Unless the soothing touch of the Almighty be upon a man's mind, he becomes the victim of his own morose thoughts. Asa knew all this, for the internment of the prophet had already been a source of constant worry. He was confronted by two alternatives. Either he could liberate the prisoner and thereby proclaim his penitence, or he must remain arrogant, brutal, and openly defiant. What a pity his knees were too stiff to bend! He had forgotten that the shortest way to heaven is to kneel. He sought the aid of his own doctors, and never did any monarch make a greater mistake.

A Great Calamity

"And Asa slept with his fathers, and died in the one and fortieth year of his reign." What a shame! This man should have lived longer. He fell a victim to his own pride. The two dates mentioned here reveal that God waited two years. He was very patient. Rejecting divine counsel, Asa chose to walk his own path, and it led to his decease. "There is a way that seemeth right unto a man, but the end thereof are the ways of death" (Prov. 14:12). Without the blessing of God, the palace had become a gaudy dwelling; the dungeon lit by the radiance of heaven was a place of quiet restfulness. Had I to follow either king or prophet, the choice would occasion no difficulty. Excellence of company can easily transform drab surroundings.

> What matters where on earth we dwell,
> On mountain top or in the dell;
> In cottage or a mansion fair?
> Where Jesus is, 'tis heaven there.

MANASSEH . . . who failed to escape from a father's prayer

(2 CHRONICLES 33:12, 13)

The promise given to the Philippian jailor ranks as one of the finest in the Bible. "Thou shalt be saved *and thine house.*" This great utterance has proved to be a source of unfailing comfort to a host of anxious people. When children persist in sinning, their Christian parents cling to the promises of God, and it is thrilling to remember God will undoubtedly keep His covenants. The story of Hezekiah and his sinful son Manasseh provides an outstanding example of this truth.

The Prayer in a Palace

Hezekiah was a man of prayer, for the greatest incidents in his life had been made memorable by intercession. When a heathen invader arrogantly sent a blasphemous letter threatening to destroy all that belonged to Israel, Hezekiah calmly took the letter into the temple and spread it out before the altar. On another occasion when he lay critically ill, he earnestly prayed for healing, and God granted to him an additional fifteen years of life. Yes, he was a man of prayer; but let it be freely admitted he never had much chance with his boy, for Manasseh was only twelve years old when his father died. The lad grew up in an atmosphere of intercession, and probably resented it. Hezekiah knew his extension of time would soon terminate, and thinking of the lad's future he surely prayed, " O God, bless and save my boy."

The Sin in the Sanctuary

"Manasseh was twelve years old when he began to reign, and . . . he did that which was evil in the sight of the Lord." It was providential that Hezekiah did not live to see the folly of his wilful son. Manasseh made a great idol, and had it erected within the sacred precincts of God's house. The observing priests probably wondered why instant judgment did not fall upon the royal blasphemer. The king recklessly proceeded from bad to worse, until " he made Jerusalem to err, and to do worse than the heathen." He insulted the prophets, and rejected their message of warning. In those days it seemed that Hezekiah had prayed in vain. His boy was a lost soul.

The Distress in a Dungeon

" And the Lord spake to Manasseh, and to his people: but they would not hearken. Wherefore the Lord brought upon them the captains of the host of the king of Assyria, which took Manasseh among the thorns, and bound him with fetters, and carried him to Babylon. And when he was in affliction, he besought the Lord his God, and humbled himself greatly before the God of his fathers." In the search for gold, man's tenacity of purpose is truly amazing. The dirty, unattractive ore is mined and brought to the surface; it is crushed, and treated in many ways until the fine yellow dust is safely in man's possession. There is another kind of gold—real gold embedded deep in the hearts of sinners. Sometimes God has to crush the human ore in order to make it yield its treasure; but since a soul is of more value than the entire world, God never hesitates to do this once the procedure becomes necessary. Manasseh sat in the darkness of his prison, and for the first time, really prayed. No cause can ever be finally lost if a man knows how to pray.

The Grave in a Garden

Here a preacher finds treasure. (i) *A great affliction led to prayer*—" In his affliction he besought the Lord." (ii) *A great answer resulted from prayer*—" God was entreated of him, and heard his supplication." (iii) *A great assurance followed prayer*—" Then Manasseh knew that the Lord He was God." (iv) *A great atonement succeeded prayer*—" And he took away the strange gods, and the idol out of the house of the Lord . . . and cast them out of the city." Manasseh's deeds proved the reality of his conversion to God. And when he died, he was buried in his own garden, where the fragrant flowers could nod in reverent salute, and where the birds could sit in the trees to sing their anthems of praise. Perhaps Israel felt it would have been wrong to take him away from home— already he had been away too long. So they dug the simple grave and buried him in the shadow of his palace. He had come home—in two senses. He was with his father, and they were both smiling.

ELIASHIB . . . who put God fi

A miracle had taken place within
city. A man named Nehemiah had
country to build again the walls of J
again it had become possible to expect
Jewish people. Long, weary years had passed since their
days of glory, and evil enemies scorned the men and women
who still talked of the greatness of Israel's history. And
then, just when it seemed that God had forgotten to be
gracious, the strange man arrived from Babylon. He
possessed letters of authority from the King of Babylon;
he had access to supplies of timber; he was wonderful!
At the meeting with the elders, Nehemiah revealed his
plans for the rebuilding of the walls, and everyone was
asked to help.

The Great Temptation

As each man moved toward his appointed portion of
the wall, the high priest stood absorbed in his thoughts.
He realized that many enemies would be ready to hinder
the great work, and through every gap in the defences
of the city, these people would come after dark to break
down the repairs and to steal from homes near their point
of entry. All around, the Israelites were repairing their
own defences, and it was perfectly understandable why
they eagerly built those parts of the wall nearest to their
own homes. The high priest probably sympathized with
them, and yet resisted the inclination to follow their
example. It was true that his own home was very much
exposed to enemy attack, and that should they invade the
city, it would be one of the first places to be destroyed.
Should he not hasten to erect that portion of the wall which
bordered on his home? The wise old man shook his head
and turned his face toward the temple. His duty was first
to God. " Then Eliashib the high priest rose up with his
brethren the priests, and they builded the sheep gate; they
sanctified it, and set up the doors of it; even unto the tower
of Meah they sanctified it, unto the tower of Hananeel."

The Great Triumph

The grand old priest realized that if he sought first the

m of God and His righteousness, all other things
be added unto him. The sheep gate probably had
se connections with that part of the sacred house where
the offerings were found, and its completion would
materially hasten the day when temple life could be
restored to normal. There would be no hope of permanent
peace and prosperity for the city until God had been
enthroned in His rightful place. The priest would have
known condemnation of spirit had he sought first his own
interests. He therefore attended to that part of the wall
intimately connected with the spiritual life of the people.
It was a noble thing to do, and in the estimation of the
watching people his soiled hands enhanced his dignity, and
his determination to guard the work increased their
admiration. Because of the danger of enemy action, with
one of his hands he wrought in the work, and with the
other hand he held a weapon (Neh. 4:17). He was far
more concerned with the erection of God's Kingdom than
with the safeguarding of his own property. Selfishness
was non-existent in his soul.

The Great Testimony

And so the work proceeded, with every man striving to
complete his portion of the wall. Sometimes the priest
thought of his own portion, but instantly dismissed any
regret that he could not attend to his own private building.
He was very wise, for God knows how to take care of
those who are loyal to Him. The third chapter of the
Book of Nehemiah supplies the record of all who
laboured on the wall, but a most significant detail demands
our consideration. In verse 20 we read, "After him
Baruch the son of Zabbai *earnestly* repaired the other
piece, from the turning of the wall unto the door of the
house of Eliashib the high priest." The word *earnestly*
stands out above all other words, for it is only used once
in describing the labours of the builders. This man
Baruch was a master-workman who put his utmost skill
into his job. He was able to build Eliashib's portion far
more competently than the priest could ever have done.
And this was God's answer to the leader's sacrificial
example. God knows how to pay His workmen, and no
one ever suffers loss through putting Him first!

JOB . . . who sailed uncharted seas

(JOB 19:25)

Within the Book of Job is a steady growth of perception unrecognized by the casual reader. The account of Job's trials is very well known, but some of his utterances provide a clear guide to his thoughts of eternal survival. Death was the impassable barrier of experience beyond which no man had been able to penetrate. Human beings were only sure of this mortal life, and should make the most of its opportunities. We do not know whether this belief was popularly shared by other people, but evidently this was his viewpoint.

How Dismal . . . death is the end of all things

As the weight of Job's burdens increased, he began to curse his day, saying, " Let the day perish wherein I was born, and the night in which it was said, There is a man child conceived " (Job 3:3). His bitterness of soul increased until suddenly he cried, I wish I were dead. " Why died I not from the womb? . . . For now should I have lain still and been quiet . . . then had I been at rest. . . . There the wicked cease from troubling; and there the weary be at rest " (3:11-17). Job preferred annihilation to pain, and declared that in death even the wicked cease from troubling. In the light of New Testament teaching, Job's conception of truth was totally wrong. Death is not the cessation of consciousness, but rather an introduction to eternal felicity or unending remorse. Alas, such teachings had never reached the soul of the ancient sufferer, and death seemed to be the great guillotine which would end his worries and his life at the same moment. We do not know how long Job remained in this place of gloom, but eventually he revealed the startling fact that his earlier views had been challenged.

How Doubtful . . . is death the end of all things ?

Job considered the great unknown and said, " If a man die, shall he live again?" He had become doubtful, and was no longer sure that the grave was a place of eternal slumber. Beyond the great barrier of mystery another world might be waiting, and there was a possibility that death may be a new beginning rather than a terminus. Job's heart had now become a place of doubt, and his utterance of 23:3-5 is among the greatest texts of the book: " Oh that I knew where I might find Him! that I might come even to His seat! I would order my cause before Him, and fill my mouth with arguments. I would know the words which He would answer me, and understand what He would say unto me." And so the process of enlightenment continued, and ultimately Job emerged into the radiance of absolute certainty concerning the problem of eternal survival.

How Decided . . . death is not the end of all things

" For I know that my Redeemer liveth, and that He shall stand at the latter day upon the earth: And though . . . worms destroy this body, yet in my flesh shall I see God." This testimony marks the greatest triumph recorded in the book. The ravages of physical decay could not hinder the miracle of resurrection— " in his flesh " he would see God. He also called God by the name " Redeemer," and this revealed another development in his personal conception of heaven's dealings with man. The law of the kinsman-redeemer stipulated that no one could redeem a slave except one who had a blood relationship with the slave. Hitherto God had been known as the Creator, but Job's prophetical eyes saw him as the Redeemer who would become " bone of our bone and flesh of our flesh." The Creator would be sent to earth, and be made in the likeness of men in order to redeem those who were under the curse of the law. *" He shall stand at the latter day upon the earth."* And with this certainty came a new approach to his most intimate problem. Now, it did not really matter that his body was a mass of putrefaction. Soon he would have a new body, for the corruptible would put on incorruption. Rejoicing in this great truth, Job said, "He knoweth the way that I take: when He hath tried me, I shall come forth as gold " (23:10). He ceased to curse his day and generation. " And the Lord turned again the captivity of Job . . . and gave Job twice as much as he had before " (42:10). Job was the first navigator to sail his soul across the uncharted sea of eternal mystery. He was a spiritual Columbus who discovered a new world.

THE YELLOW DOVES ... bought in a second-hand shop

(PSALM 68:13)

"Though ye have lien among the pots, yet shall ye be as the wings of a dove covered with silver, and her feathers with yellow gold." One of the most charming Old Testament pictures seems to lie behind this text. During the reign of King David, a bird-cage could be seen standing in the window of an ancient second-hand shop. An assortment of household articles probably occupied most of the window space, but in among the pots and pans was a cage with its feathered captives. A bird lover one day visited the place, in order to purchase the birds and set them free. He carried them into the sunshine, and allowed them to fly away. As they turned in the air their yellow wings shone in the sunshine and appeared to be made of the finest gold. David knew about this incident, and mentioned it in one of his psalms. He likened the nation to the captive doves, and went on to suggest that although Israel had been among the pots and pans of Egypt's bondage, God's strong arm had redeemed them. Exultantly he sang, "He that is our God is the God of salvation."

The Captives and the Cage

Two types of doves might easily have been in the cage. Some birds had been born in captivity, and had never known the freedom of the open hills. They had always gazed at prison bars, and knew nothing of the existence of a vast world of sunshine and open spaces. Other birds had been trapped and brought into captivity, where their memories of former folly increased their discomfiture. They had left their rightful sphere, and in search of tempting morsels had descended to an earthly realm of danger. A trap had closed about them, and their captivity had commenced. These two types were different from each other, in that the former had no knowledge of the world in which its mate had once lived. The birds in the cage clearly resemble the sinner and the backslider sitting side by side in the bondage of sin. The first type—born in sin and shapen in iniquity—has never known the freedom of the sons of God; the second type once revelled in such liberty, but, alas, through sin has fallen again into bondage.

The Purchaser and the Price

The scene in the old shop was remarkably interesting. The bird lover had no thought of cages, and his attitude probably bewildered the shopkeeper. We do not know the amount of money paid for the release of the captives, but in any case the buyer considered it to be money well spent. In *The Land and the Book*, Dr. Thomson describes the pitiable cry of the yellow dove, and even declares that it became more than he could bear. The unknown bird lover heard the same kind of cry, and it won his heart. Had he ignored its appeal he would have been troubled for ever. If the doves remind us of human souls held captive in sin, we must now seek the spiritual identity of the purchaser.

> Somebody came and lifted me
> Out of my sin and misery;
> Somebody came, oh, who could it be?
> Who could it be, but Jesus.

The Saviour left the ivory palaces of heaven to walk down our street of woe, and with His own precious blood He redeemed us from sin.

The Songsters and the Sky

The birds were probably very frightened, and wondered what strange fate was about to overwhelm them; but when they were carried into the sunshine and thrown high in the air, their dreams suddenly became true. They stretched their wings, and feeling the upward lift of the wind, they gained confidence and climbed higher into the sunshine. Their feathers shone like gold as the limitless heavens opened to receive them. Their term of bondage had ended; their cries of mourning were replaced by notes of real joy. *They were free!* The songs of the birds have been translated into human experience, for there are countless thousands of people who are able to repeat: " If the Son shall make you free, ye shall be free indeed." It may appear strange that the King of Israel should be interested in captive birds; but it is far more surprising that the King of heaven should be interested in us.

THE SINGERS . . . who lost their music in a sea of sorrow

Within the fifty-six mile circular wall of Babylon stood the greatest city of the ancient world. Its ornamental palaces and picturesque hanging gardens were destined to become world famous. Its armies had triumphed over the surrounding nations, and the king sat at ease amid scenes of unparalleled splendour. Somewhere along the banks of the river the unfortunate Israelites had erected their pitiable hovels where, at the end of the toilsome days, they sat beneath starry heavens and thought of home. Long afterward one wrote, " By the rivers of Babylon, there we sat down, yea, we wept, when we remembered Zion. We hanged our harps upon the willows in the midst thereof. For there they that carried us away captive required of us a song; and they that wasted us required of us mirth, saying, Sing us one of the songs of Zion."

The Singers who Wept

" How shall we sing the Lord's song in a strange land?" Alas, the memories of home hurt, for they reminded the captives of days when the prophet of God had been scorned, and his message rejected. Then, a passionate desire to worship idols had over-ruled all faithfulness to Jehovah, and in rebellion the people of Israel had ruined themselves. Now, alone and helpless in a foreign land, they sat and grieved. Some had gained favour in the heathen court, but the great mass of the people were abject slaves, whose cause seemed utterly lost. They had even lost their God—or so it seemed; and the hopelessness of their case filled them with despair.

The Saviour who Waited

Many of the people had been born in captivity, and stories of the greatness of Israel's God suggested scorn. They would ask, " Where is He now? Has He forgotten to be gracious?" Adversity can easily blind one's eyes to the nearness of the Almighty. During this time of Israel's great sorrow, He was actually with them in Babylon— waiting and watching the sore travail through which the soul of a nation would be born anew. Love and wisdom are co-equal in the heart of the Infinite; but God can never do much for any man until self is dethroned. Sometimes He has to appear cruel and forgetful in order to display the wonder of His healing grace. He waited forty years to bring Egypt out of Israel; He waited seventy years to bring Babylon out of Israel; and we might ask how long He has already waited for us.

The Souls who Worshipped

He did not wait in vain. Through the anguish and despair of Israel, a new determination struggled for expression. When the arrogant king of the heathen commanded his subjects to bow before the great image set up in the plains of Dura, three Hebrew boys adamantly refused. Their actions seemed suicidal, but they had decided that even death would be preferable to dishonour. They had little hope that the God of their fathers would save them, but in any case, they would never serve idols. Had their forefathers been men of this calibre, the nation would have avoided disaster. In spite of great danger, another Hebrew opened his window and prayed toward Jerusalem. No case can ever be quite hopeless when men know how to pray, especially when they pray with their windows open!

The Salvation so Wonderful

Belshazzar the king summoned a thousand of his lords, and held a most blasphemous party. His deliberation in calling for the vessels of Jehovah called aloud to high heaven for judgment. He cared not. Then came the hand, writing his doom on the wall (Dan. 5:5-28), and that night the Medio-Persians took the city. It is said they dug a new course for the bed of the river, and by turning the waters revealed the one flaw in the defences of Babylon. They swarmed beneath the water-gates, and brought liberation to the captives. Israel's mourning was turned to joy, and they exultantly cried, " When the Lord turned again the captivity of Israel, we were like them that dream." Their prayers had been heard, and their sickness of soul healed. How refreshing it is to remember that the God who lived in those days, is just the same to-day.

SOLOMON . . . and the girl who said " No "

(SONG OF SOLOMON 5:1-16)

It is strange that many Bible teachers in their exposition of the Song of Solomon cite Solomon as a type of Christ. To say the least, it needs great imagination to visualize the lustful monarch of Israel as a forerunner of the incomparable Bridegroom, and we are glad that the Scriptures suggest a far happier interpretation of this choice story. Here we have the eternal triangle—the tale of two men and a girl. During the closing period of David's life, it was considered necessary to find a beautiful girl who would act as nurse for her royal master. Abishag the Shunammite was therefore brought to the palace, where the princes fell madly in love with her. It is most suggestive that, when on behalf of her son, Adonijah's mother sought her hand in marriage, Solomon angrily exclaimed, " And why dost thou ask Abishag the Shunammite for Adonijah? ask for him the kingdom also. . . . As the Lord liveth, Adonijah shall be put to death this day " (1 Kings 2:21-24). Solomon was the great conqueror of women, yet he who possessed the daughter of Pharaoh, became singularly attracted to this fair maiden of Israel. His interest was intensified when she resisted his advances. She already loved a man—a shepherd of Israel.

The Visitor in the Dark . . . love calling

We see the home close by the vineyard. It was a palace where Abishag reigned as queen of her own domain. Undoubtedly she often thought of her old surroundings, where a shepherd boy cursed the day when David's seekers had found and taken away his sweetheart. Solomon offered wealth, enjoyment, dancing, music; alas, he only offered affection, a simple homestead, the song of the birds, and the freedom of the hills. Yet the heart of the shepherd yearned for his beloved, and one night he stole away to her new home. Abishag listened to his whispered callings, and admitted to herself, " I sleep, but my heart waketh: it is the voice of my beloved that knocketh, saying, Open to me, my sister, my love, my dove, my undefiled: for my head is filled with dew, and my locks with the drops of the night " (5:2). She shrugged

75

her shoulders, and exercised care in hiding her true feelings. She answered, " I have put off my coat; how shall I put it on? I have washed my feet; how shall I defile them?"—I have retired to bed; to dress again will be an awful bore. Couldn't you come at some other time? Stupid girl, your beauty exceeded your wisdom!

The Vision at the Door . . . love pleading

" My beloved put in his hand by the hole in the door, and my heart was moved for him " (v. 4). This is easily understood. No girl can give her heart to two men. She saw his hand outstretched in mute pleading, and the depth of her being was stirred. Is it possible that she recognized there the scars of some earlier misfortune? In any case, that hand struck chords deep in her soul, and the resultant music thrilled her. He loved her; he desired her. " I rose up to open to my beloved . . . my hands dropped sweet smelling myrrh upon the handles of the lock. I opened to my beloved; but my beloved had withdrawn himself and was gone " (vv. 5, 6). Yes, silly girl, you kept him waiting; you deserve your fate.

The Victory in the Dawn . . . love winning

" I sought him, but I could not find him. . . . The watchmen that went about the city found me, they smote me. . . . I charge you, O daughters of Jerusalem, if ye find my beloved, that ye tell him, that I am sick of love " (vv. 6-8). Obviously the maidens of the city could not comprehend such devotion, for they answered, " What is thy beloved more than another beloved, O thou fairest among women? " (v. 9). Such an answer would never have been given had Solomon been the unhappy suitor. And thus she went forth into the streets to seek her shepherd-lover, and as the rising sun tipped the eastern sky with radiance, they were reunited. When Solomon heard the story, he was so impressed that he enshrined the details in his immortal sonnet.

We think of another Shepherd—the Good Shepherd, who competes with the prince of this world for the hand of His fair Church. It is one of the evidences of divine inspiration that wheresoever one turns in Holy Scripture, the seeing eye can easily discern Christ.

JEHOIAKIM ... who burned his Bıble

(JEREMIAH 36:23)

It is a dangerous thing to reject the message of God; it is fatal to attempt its destruction. Jehoiakim the king of Judah did this, and brought upon himself inescapable doom. In this sad story we find three momentous scenes, and three vital truths. We shall consider them in that order.

Scene 1

Jeremiah sat in his simple home, dictating to his servant the message of God. Nothing disturbed the silence except the scratching of the quill with which the scribe fulfilled his duties. To-morrow the people would throng the temple, and God's latest message must be written in time for the service. The prophet continued his dictation, and finally the manuscript was completed. Barak drew his chair to the fireside and repeated aloud what he had written, so that his master might be assured the words had been faithfully recorded. As stillness settled upon the room, both men thought of the coming day and realized that the proclamation of the message would have repercussions in every part of the nation. Ultimately Jeremiah commissioned his servant for the great task, and as Barak quietly withdrew, the prophet was left alone with his God.

Scene 2

The temple was filled with worshippers when, amid great silence, Barak unrolled his parchment and read the latest predictions of his master Jeremiah. His " Thus saith the Lord " rang ominously through the sanctuary, and his forecast of impending doom sent a shudder through the souls of the listeners. Even the priests stood as men horrified. The reading ended, a general hubbub shattered the silence of the temple, and from the crowd of clamouring people a young nobleman rushed to inform the king of the latest development in the spiritual history of the nation.

Scene 3

The king sat in his winter house, where a fire brightly burned on the hearth. Around him sat his friends, whose morals were not above reproach. They listened to the voice of a young man, Jehudi, who slowly read the prophet's message. Suddenly the king contemptuously snatched the manuscript, and after a cursory glance at it, he cut it in pieces and threw it into the flames. Thus he expressed to his friends that he cared neither for God nor His prophet. Within a few days he was dead.

PROPOSITION 1. *Judgment is always prefaced by warning grace.*

The sin of man may be exceedingly great, but the mercy of God will surely warn him before it becomes too late to repent. The sinner may continue his path of evil, but will never be able to say, " I never had a chance." The divine warning may come in various ways—through sickness, bereavement, or through the preaching of the Gospel. Man's destiny will be decided by his attitude in those moments of grace.

PROPOSITION 2. *Judgment is always merited by unreasoning action.*

A sick man invites disaster when he persistently rejects the advice of his doctor, and if through his own stupidity he should die, blame can be attached to none but himself. And this is equally true in regard to spiritual health. When sinners reject the warnings of God, their attitude foreruns eternal tragedy. Jehoiakim never sought a meeting with God's servant; neither did he pause to reason. It became obvious to him that he could either repent of his sin or continue in his self-pleasing ways. His action was inexcusable when without preliminary thought, he violently destroyed God's word.

PROPOSITION 3. *Judgment always ends in inescapable doom.*

Justice and mercy are co-equal in the heart of God. Neither one suffers at the hand of the other. God's love delights in offering mercy; His holiness demands the observance of justice. These are the basic principles of all divine dealings with man. Man must accept or reject God's great word; and according to his actions, so also will God eventually deal with man. Jehoiakim perished, and will have all eternity in which to remember his folly. We shall be very foolish if we follow in his footsteps.

THE HEBREW BOYS . . . who met Christ in a fire (Daniel 3:25)

In regard to the person of Christ, there are three schools of thought. To many people He is just a figure of history —someone who lived and died nearly 2,000 years ago. To others, He is the mystical figure who reigns in the distant heavens. To the third class, He is a living bright reality, a personal Saviour who dwells and reigns in human hearts. Ordinary people are apt to view with suspicion all who claim such intimacy with the Saviour, for to them, such words savour of fanaticism. Yet there are multitudes of these radiant people, whose charm and power are undeniable. If it be possible for Christ to become real in a man's experience, it will be profitable to inquire how this may be realized. The answer is clearly supplied in the Book of Daniel.

Their Character

Seventy years in a foreign land! Seventy years of cruel slavery! How awful! We sympathize with the Hebrew captives who languished in the service of the Babylonians. We understand why they sat beneath the starry heavens and wept as they thought of home. Many of them had been born in captivity, and their conception of God was rather confused. Yet in spite of doubt and prejudice, their knowledge of God and the law had been preserved. Old men taught the children, and the teaching bore fruit in the lives of the scholars. When some of the boys were later asked to conform to the customs of the heathen, to drink the accursed wine and to partake of the forbidden food, they resolutely refused. There is no evidence to prove they had any personal acquaintance with God, but the teaching of earlier days had formulated character strong enough to resist evil.

Their Cry

The king sat moodily in his palace; superstition played havoc with his peace of mind. He had forgotten a dream. He had presented the magicians with a most unreasonable request. He had informed them that unless they discovered and interpreted the lost mystery, they would be executed.

They had failed, and more than ever his mind had become the prey of his superstitious fears. The time of execution had drawn nigh. Outside the palace, the Hebrews desperately prayed to the God of heaven, and their prayers were answered. The dream was revealed to Daniel, and thus was the realization of the reality of God brought a little nearer.

Their Confession

There is still no evidence that they had enjoyed an experience of the personal presence of God. They had prayed to the distant God of their fathers, and Jehovah had heard their cry. The story moves onward. The king was excited and thrilled, for to-morrow in the plains of Dura the vast concourse of his people would bow before the image. Everyone would bow—or so he thought. Three captives sat in their simple abode and discussed their attitude to the king's edict. The moment had come when to remain a secret follower of Jehovah would be impossible. It would be necessary to make public their confession of faith, and this policy would be fraught with great danger. Their decision was never in doubt.

Their Companion

The deed is done; the king is angry. " Is it true that ye do not serve my gods? . . . ye shall be cast into the midst of a burning fiery furnace, and who is that God who shall deliver you out of my hands?" The prisoners gave their answer, and " then was Nebuchadnezzar full of fury, and the form of his countenance was changed. . . . Then these men were . . . cast into the midst of the burning fiery furnace." But the king " rose up in haste . . . and said. . . . Did not we cast three men bound into the midst of the fire? . . . Lo, I see four men . . . and the form of the fourth is like *the Son of God.*" Thus Christ became real in the experience of the three young men. They had believed in the historical God even when they attended the classes of the elders; they had believed in the God of heaven when their prayers had been answered; but now God had become intimately real—He was with them in the fire. Such joys would have remained unknown had they been too ashamed to confess publicly their allegiance to Him. And as it was, so it is (Rom. 10:9).

JONAH . . . who ran away from God

(JONAH 1:1-3)

Three suggestions have been made to explain Jonah's disobedience to God. (i) He was a bigoted Jew who refused to have any dealings with a Gentile city. (ii) He was a coward, and feared the brutality of the people to whom he was commissioned to preach. (iii) He was a very brave man, who loved his nation more than he loved his own life. It has been said that he feared the warlike intentions of the Ninevites, and realized that the only safeguard for Israel was the annihilation of this great people.

His Brave Disobedience

No true conception of this story can be possible unless first we appreciate the consequences of such a rash act. The law of God stated that if the watchman refused to warn the people of approaching danger, their blood would be required at his hand. When Jonah deliberately turned his back upon the appointed task and fled from the presence of the Lord, he realized he was fleeing into eternal condemnation. Under law he was sacrificing his soul. And this vital fact seems to answer the claims of the first two suggestions put forth. It is extremely doubtful whether a man's exclusiveness would rise to such heights of self-sacrifice; and in the second place, it required a great deal more courage to run into the eternal shadows than it did to face the persecution of a Ninevite mob.

His Belated Decision

It has been ascertained by archæologists that the Ninevites of Jonah's day were actively engaged in warlike preparations against Israel. Jonah apparently knew this, and feared the outcome of their aggression. If the judgment of God obliterated the city, the threatened invasion would not take place, and Israel would be saved. If the people repented of their sin, God would spare them, and at some future date Israel would have to endure their tyranny. Jonah was perfectly correct, for within fifty years of his refusal to preach to these people, they pillaged Israel and caused untold havoc. The prophet was not alone in his love for Israel. Moses had offered to have his name removed from God's book if only the people could be spared; and even Paul wished that he could become a castaway for Israel's sake. When Jonah was cast from the storm-tossed boat he fell into the arms of God, and in the uncanny experiences of the following days he knew the impossibility of fleeing beyond the reach of God. Jonah prayed and promised, saying, "I will sacrifice unto thee with the voice of thanksgiving; I will pay that that I have vowed" (2:9). And the Lord knew that the conflict was over, and "spake unto the fish, and it vomited out Jonah upon the dry land."

His Bold Declaration

The supernatural signs attending the preaching of Jonah were astonishing, and called for some explanation. His solitary sermon was followed by unparalleled scenes of repentance, and it became obvious that something strange had taken place. The Ninevites worshipped Dagon, the fish-god, and here in their midst was one who had apparently been delivered from the grave. His message demanded urgent consideration. They therefore repented in sackcloth and ashes. And the preacher who should have been the proudest man in the world, was instantly filled with dismay. Becoming angry, he prayed, "O Lord, was not this my saying when I was yet in my country? Therefore I fled before unto Tarshish, *for I knew that thou art a gracious God, and merciful . . . and of great kindness. . . ."*

His Bewildering Despair

"Therefore now, O Lord, take, I beseech thee, my life from me; for it is better for me to die than to live." Then, hoping that some tragedy might befall the city, he went out to sit on the outskirts of the place "till he might see what would become of the city." "And God said, Doest thou well to be angry?" The subsequent story is so well known that it only remains to say that, although Jonah, Moses, and Paul, were willing to sacrifice themselves on behalf of Israel, the Lord graciously spared His willing servants. There was Another who was also willing to make the supreme sacrifice, and God permitted Him to do so. "God . . . spared not his own son, but delivered him up for us all . . ." (Rom. 8:32).

THE WISE MEN ... who looked through a starry window

The Bethlehem story is the greatest in literature, and yet how different is man's conception of it from that which actually took place. Two thousand years ago, in a hastily prepared cave and without any medical assistance whatsoever, a young woman gave birth to her son. There were no picturesque surroundings and twinkling lights such as those so ornamentally presented on the Christmas cards, for probably the only illumination present came from a simple lamp, and the light of motherhood just beginning to shine in Mary's eyes. Yet in spite of the unpretentious birthplace, the story of His coming will never grow old.

God Revealing the Son

As we consider the manger scene, three vital truths become obvious. (i) *God is never indifferent to human need.* Four centuries had passed since the appearance of a prophet, and there were people in Israel who were tempted to think that God had forsaken His people; that their sufferings and prayers were meaningless to Him. God's response to this problem was found in the Bethlehem story. (ii) *The Lord Jesus is God's answer to human need.* In the fullness of time God sent forth His Son, to be born of a woman; and since this was His only-begotten Son, should He fail, there can be no other. The divine remedy for human ill is the Saviour. (iii) *If God sent His Son, the implications of such an act are far too great to escape attention.* The God responsible for such a gift must at least make known the glad story. How futile will be the coming of Christ if the world remains in ignorance of the fact.

Greatness Recognizing the Son

Since the Gospel was first to the Jew, it was perfectly reasonable that the initial announcement of His coming should be made to the shepherds. Yet the tidings of God's love can never be confined within the narrow limits of one nation. Thus far away to the east, an astronomer looked intently at the sky, for to his practised eye the appearance of a new comet revealed great mystery. He and others

83

of his type read in the brilliance the news that somewhere a king had been born. It is not for us to speculate how they arrived at this conclusion; it is sufficient for us to know that God is able to speak every man's language. We are not told how many of these eminent men made the pilgrimage to Bethlehem; nor do we know if they all came from the same district. Yet other things are known. (i) *They saw grace in the sky.* God had graciously revealed His purposes. (ii) *They saw guidance in the star.* This logically follows, for of what use would it be to tell men of the Christ unless some means be found whereby they can be led to Him? (iii) *They saw God in the Son,* and placed their choicest treasures at His feet. The memory of that glorious vision enriched them for ever.

Guilt Resisting the Son

Unerringly the star led them over the hills and through the valleys, but as they drew near to the city of Jerusalem their guide suddenly disappeared. The wise men were thereupon obliged to seek information regarding the birthplace of the new king, and thus the news reached Herod and his people. We must ask the reason for this break in the sequence of guidance. Surely the star could have led the pilgrims until they finally reached their destination. Why should there be a delay in Jerusalem? It is God's will that all men should hear of Christ. He cannot make men yield to the Lord Jesus, but His is the responsibility of carrying the message to them. After their visit to the palace the wise men rejoiced, for the star reappeared to guide them on the final stage of their journey. King Herod sat alone with his problems, and the tragic stages of his increasing sinfulness are clearly defined. (i) *His fear.* The coming of another king presented a new challenge to his own throne. God's king would never take second place. (ii) *His faith.* He sought information in the Scriptures, and by so doing increased his condemnation. He would never be able to plead ignorance as an excuse for his sin. (iii) *His folly.* Thwarted, he fought grimly against the advent of the child Jesus, and in so doing he sealed his fate. He died a poor, broken sinner, having lost the glorious opportunity of writing his name in history. He might have been known as the additional wise man.

THE MAN . . . who vanished

There is an apparent discrepancy between the accounts of Matthew and Luke in regard to the deliverance of the Gadarene demoniac. Matthew firmly insists there were two demoniacs awaiting the coming of Christ. Luke does not deny the presence of the second man, but is content to tell the story of the one. For some unknown reason the second man failed to reappear, and we are left wondering what happened to him. Your guess is as good as mine, but if we share our thoughts we might discover truth.

Was He Forgetful?

He could never forget the wonderful moment when the Saviour brought relief from inward horror. Yet in his thrilling excitement, did he rush to his home and loved ones; and in the tranquillity of the new calm, did he forget the One who had rescued him from the storm? If this were the case, he resembles many modern people. Men and even nations are apt to flee to God in their distresses. Prolonged periods of prayer are the usual means to win from God those things most desired. Yet in the triumph of subsequent days both man and nation are prone to forget their indebtedness, and to return to ways of sin. Some of us could hardly blame the demoniac.

Was He Fearful?

Some unknown farmer had lost a complete herd of two thousand swine. The savings of years had vanished in a moment. He would not be pleased. There would be no compensation, and after due consideration he would have many things to say. If other people were involved in the loss, then quite a number of impoverished citizens would give vent to their anger. Was the healed demoniac scared of the charges that might be brought against him, and as a result did he stay in hiding? Who can tell? It is at least a possible solution, and no one can deny that such calculated action may still be witnessed. There are many people who recognize their indebtedness to Christ, and secretly acknowledge that they ought publicly to confess their allegiance; yet they shrink from open discipleship.

Fearful of what people might say, they remain secret disciples. Their example is not good.

Did His Family Interfere?

It would have been most natural had he returned to his home, to share the great news of his deliverance. Probably he had been estranged from his people for a considerable time. The coming of Christ opened up new possibilities; home and family were once again within reach. We could never blame him for his action in going to them; we are concerned with his failure to return later in thankfulness to the Master. Did his family talk him out of this idea? Were his objections overcome by the persuasion of his own kith and kin? Alas, man has always been failing at this point. Perhaps we shall never know how many people have secretly said, " Lord, I will follow thee, but let me first go bid them farewell which are at home at my house "—and then have vanished from the scene.

Did the Future Trouble Him?

If this were the case, we are able to appreciate his difficulties. He would know that Christ had a band of disciples. Had they not been present that same morning? Would the Saviour make great demands in return for His act of delivering grace? Would He expect the former demoniac to forsake all and to follow whithersoever He might lead? And greatest of all the problems, would the convert be able to maintain such high and holy standards of life and service? Was he afraid to come near to Jesus lest he should be confronted with these demands? People still excuse their staying away from Christ. They say, " I could never live that life; I should fail." This sounds sincere, but actually it lacks reality. Our starting point for deliberation should be what He has already done for us, and not what He might yet require. To try and fail is at least more satisfactory than never to try at all. The demoniac lived ever after with a guilty conscience. Poor fellow.

THE HOUSEHOLDER . . . who fought with a devil
(MATTHEW 12:43-45)

This Scripture belongs to one of the most fascinating of the Lord's sermons. Christ was a great student of human nature, and it is said of Him that He did not commit Himself unto the people because He knew all men. Constantly He came face to face with all types, and here in this challenging message He centres attention on one class—the man who says he could never live the Christian life even though he tried.

The Parable

The house was a study in contrasts. It seemed impossible that this could be one home, for its two ends were two extremes. One was as beautiful as the other was ugly. Seen through modern eyes, one end was charmingly decorated, beautifully curtained, and a sight to gladden the heart. The other was bleak and barren and exceedingly dirty. *But it was one house.* The good householder occupied one portion, and a devil occupied the other. The good man desired to throw out his evil neighbour, but felt unequal to the task. They continued to live side by side. We are reminded of a human heart where so often the good and bad impulses live together. Paul said, " When I would do good, evil is present with me " ; and Studdart Kennedy once wrote,

> There's summat that pulls us up,
> And summat that pulls us down;
> And the consequence is that we wobble
> 'Twixt muck and a golden crown.

If we could only be rid of the evil within us, our entire house could be beautified according to our noblest desires.

The Problem

A great inspiration energized the householder, and in one supreme moment of triumph he ejected the unwanted devil. Probably he was more surprised than the evil one, but after a little while the devil said, " I will return into my house from whence I came out." Then he discovered it to be empty, swept, and garnished; and realizing that the householder might expel him once again, he took with him seven other spirits more wicked than himself. Thus, said Christ, "the last state of that man was worse than the first." There is something peculiarly suggestive about this scene. It is obvious that Christ appreciated the difficulties of sincere souls. It seems so futile to make any decision which in after days might return as a boomerang to create dismay. It is easy at times to cry, "Lord, I will follow thee whithersoever thou goest," and yet to fail when subsequently the road is long and steep. In the glorious ecstasy of His presence we can brave unlimited perils; but, alas, we are mindful that the expelled demon might some day return with reinforcements. Our philosophy says, "Better be content with the presence of one devil than run the risk of his bringing seven others."

The Preaching

The weakness of the story seems to be in that, having expelled the demon, *the householder was content to live alone.* If he could have found a companion whose power exceeded that of many devils, he would have had a chance of maintaining the freedom of his home. And however imaginative this may seem, it is nevertheless the real fact behind this message. In verses 22-24 we are told of the deliverance of a demoniac, and no one could deny the actuality of the miracle. Even His enemies admitted He had performed the impossible, but they cunningly suggested He was in league with Beelzebub, the prince of the devils. But let us remember that He had established beyond all doubt His superiority over demons. He thereupon proceeded to describe the harassed householder, and to this there can only be one feasible explanation. If such a man could invite Christ to live in his heart, he would find security in the new fellowship. And that is the crux of the Gospel message. If the Lord tarries with me, His strength will be made perfect in my weakness. How silly it is to live in the shadow of nameless fears. I must seek the companionship of the new Guest.

KING HEROD . . . the only man to whom Christ refused to speak

(MATTHEW 14:10; LUKE 23:9)

The royal ballroom was hushed. Uneasy stillness reigned supreme as a host of guests watched a startled king. Herod, the fool, the tipsy monarch, had been sobered by the amazing request of a dancing girl. The swirl of her flimsy skirts, the rhythm of her swaying body, the excitement of the dance, had rushed him into entanglements. Feverishly he had cried, " Ask what you will, and you shall have it, to the half of my kingdom " ; and now, equally as feverishly, he wished he had been a wiser man.

A King Remembering

The girl waited; the guests waited; and downstairs in a dirty dungeon sat the peaceful prophet of God, the brave John Baptist whose head the girl had claimed. Every moment seemed endless, and suddenly a sickly smile spread over Herod's debauched face as he gave his command. A little later, when the executioner had presented the gory prize, the dancing girl stumbled out to her sinful mother, and the guests resumed their festivities. Probably alone in the crowd, alone with his nameless fears, Herod knew that for him at least the birthday had ended. He had fought a battle. Either his pride or his prisoner had had to die. His decision could never be rescinded. He had seen the face of the murdered man, and would never forget it. It would haunt him for ever. When he heard of another prophet, he anxiously asked questions; and then, brushing aside all other opinions, he fearfully said, " This is John Baptist; he is risen from the dead." And each night he half expected a ghost to exact vengeance. He knew how impossible it was to escape the attentions of a guilty conscience.

A King Rebuked

With the passing of the months the strain of fear eased, and when Herod had the opportunity of seeing the new Teacher his peace of mind was restored immediately. Contemptuously his lip curled as he heard of new exploits, and ultimately some of his hirelings came to announce that, as Herod had dealt with the first prophet, so also would he deal with the second. Contrary to expectation, the Lord did not run away. Alas, Herod the fearful murderer had become Herod the cynic. Assured of temporary safety from any ghostly visitation, he proceeded on another murderous escapade. It is far easier to step on the path of sin than it is to leave it. All thoughts of the future had been forgotten. Herod was enjoying himself, and nothing else mattered. That his soul might be lost never even occurred to him. Jesus said, " Go ye and tell that fox . . . I shall be perfected."

A King Rejected

The months passed by, and Herod came to Jerusalem. He was pleased indeed as he held in his hand a message from Pilate. The Governor would be sending around a prisoner—Jesus. Ah! Jesus, the healer who performed miracles. This would make great entertainment for the evening. " Officer, bring him in." We cannot tell how long Jesus was required to stay, but His unbroken silence during all the time of questioning cries aloud for explanation. His two eyes must have burned as fire into the conscience of the king who taunted Him, and ultimately Herod sent Him back whence He had come. It is tragic that He who could die for sinners should never speak a word to warn this one. Here was a man heading for judgment, and the Lord Jesus made no attempt to save him. Soon afterward Herod toppled from his throne, and before much could be done, his soul had gone into the darkness. He had sinned away his chances, for on his soul lay the blood of John Baptist. God once said, " My spirit shall not always strive with man." There is an end to all things, even the offer of mercy. Herod exchanged his soul for the plaudits of men. " Nevertheless for the oath's sake, *and them which sat with him at meat* he commanded John's head to be given her " (Matt. 14:9). It seemed a fair exchange—but he lost on the deal.

THE SYROPHENICIAN . . . who tried to deceive Christ

How strange it seems that Jesus only went once to certain places; and how suggestive that always the solitary visit led to something supernatural. For example, He arrived in Nain in time to meet a funeral and heal a broken heart. In Tyre and Sidon, where apparently His voice had never been heard, He—but let the story speak for itself. Somewhere in the vicinity a Gentile mother lived with her stricken daughter—one possessed with a devil. Periodically her yearning eyes watched the people going away to the southern towns where the great Healer would be preaching. How she longed to accompany them; but alas, she was needed at home. When the travellers returned she would ask for news of the meetings, and her eyes would shine with amazement when she heard of the miracles He had performed. "And Jesus," she would ask, "is He a Jew?"

"Oh, yes, and He always works among the people of the chosen race." She remembered the existent racial barriers, and sighing, she half whispered, "What a pity He's not a Gentile; then perhaps I could have gone to Him."

How Great the Lord's Perception

When she heard that Jesus was about to visit the district, her desires to see Him became irrepressible, and as she remembered Jewish prejudice she faced her greatest temptation. She could speak Hebrew, and probably looked like many of the Jewish ladies. He might not detect the deception. Anyhow, it was worth trying; and for her daughter's sake, she went forth with the cry of a Jewess. "O Lord, thou son of David, have mercy on me; my daughter is grievously vexed with a devil. But He answered her not a word." His indifference must have seemed catastrophic to this misguided little mother, for she had yet to learn that all who come to Christ must be honest. Let us be careful to deal kindly with her. She did not know that within the circle of God's fatherly care all racial barriers disappear. She was dishonest, and the Lord Jesus knew.

91

How Great the Lord's Patience

The embarrassed disciples must have found His attitude most awkward; it was so contradictory of all they had ever known of Him. The crowd also must have been greatly surprised, and finally the disciples whispered, " Send her away, for she crieth after us." He replied, " I am not sent but unto the lost sheep of the house of Israel." The patriots would nod approval; but desperately the woman fell at His feet, crying, " Lord, help me."

Ah! kindly little soul, you are doing this for the girl's sake; but you are still wrong. You seem to be saying, " If you have come for the lost sheep of the house of Israel, why not help me?" The Lord Jesus patiently waited for her enlightenment to come. He still does when His people are difficult.

How Great the Lord's Power

" It is not meet to take the children's bread and to cast it to dogs." Oh, surely the warmth of His eyes offset the seeming rebuke of His lips! Momentarily shocked, she could only stare at Him; but ultimately she replied, " Truth, Lord: yet the dogs eat of the crumbs which fall from their master's table"—I may be a Gentile, a dog; but is there not a portion for me? Of course, little lady, there is a portion for all when we come honestly. Listen to the Lord's word, " O woman, great is thy faith: be it unto thee even as thou wilt," and now hurry home, your little girl is well and waiting for you.

As she went the Lord Jesus turned, and before long His voice was heard again in the familiar haunts of Galilee. But—and this fact must always be remembered—He had been once at least to Tyre and Sidon. He did not go in vain. To-night He might come to us. Let us be ready.

THE CROWD . . . that knelt down and reached Heaven
(MATTHEW 15:30)

The silvery waves were breaking on Galilee's beaches, and the fishermen were probably mending their nets when Jesus drew near and "went up into the mountain and sat down there." Many of the men had already met the great Teacher, and would instantly recognize Him. They left their work, and spreading the news in the homes of the people, they brought their sick folk and "cast them down at Jesus' feet; and He healed them." The congregation on the ancient hillside seems strangely like the people of to-day.

The Blind Man

Somewhere in the village he sat in his world of darkness. He could hear the voices of other people, and to some degree understood what they were trying to describe. Yet he was unable to see. On that remarkable morning someone told him of Jesus, and explained that this was the great Prophet who could open the eyes of the blind. He had only to come and in simple faith respond to the Teacher's message, and all would be well. Yet to this man in the dark, the project was not as easy as it first appeared to be. He could not see, and was expected to accept the testimony of other people. This was asking much. Was the story true? And that picture presents the case of every unconverted soul. Friends may bring a radiant testimony of Christ's power to save; they may describe the joy of God's salvation; but to a poor sinner this can sound confusing and uncertain. Yet when he can be persuaded to draw near to Christ, and above all else, to kneel at the feet of Jesus, his eyes will be opened and he will joyfully exclaim, "The half was never told me."

The Lame Man

Poor fellow! His legs were very troublesome. Once he had walked perfectly, but of late years he had been obliged to use crutches. His eyesight was good; and he required no explanation of things beyond the reach of his vision. Yet carelessness had probably robbed him of freedom of movement. Unwittingly he had placed his foot in some

93

place of danger, and suddenly losing his balance, had fallen. From that moment he was lame. He hobbled to the outskirts of the crowd and stood listening to the message of Christ. His name was Mr. Backslider! No man of his type ever needs persuasion concerning the truth of the Gospel message; he knows it already. The trouble is in his feet! Self-confidently he forgot the injunction, "Let him that thinketh he standeth take heed lest he fall," and placing his foot in a worldly pot-hole he lost his balance, and has never been the same since. In fact, his life would be most miserable if he were denied the support of his crutches. He would agree that these are poor substitutes for strong legs, but they are better than nothing. "Poor backslider! Why don't you kneel at the Saviour's feet? He is a marvellous Physician."

The Dumb Man

How easy it is to recognize this man as he silently stands in the crowd. His eyesight is good; and because he has exercised care in his daily walk, he is not lame. He is neither the unbeliever nor the backslider; he is the secret disciple, who has never made a public confession of Christ. Let us watch him as he wrestles with his great problem. Should he kneel at the Saviour's feet? How would he be able to pray? Would Christ understand; and what would the watching people say? Oh dear! We shall never know what battles had to be fought before this man knelt on the mountainside. Then he quickly discovered the ability of Jesus to hear the unspoken prayer of a man's appealing eyes. "And the tongue of the dumb was loosed."

The Maimed, and Many Others

The maimed, who had been injured in life's encounters; the many others, who might have included people just like us; they all knelt at the feet of Jesus, and no one knelt in vain. And the greatest news in the world is that Christ is just the same to-day. How futile will be all our efforts if we fail to reach this place of blessing.

> Down at the Saviour's feet,
> Love finds its heaven all complete;
> Burdens roll away,
> Night is turned to day,
> Down at the Saviour's feet.

MARY ... who brought her flowers *before* Christ died

(MATTHEW 26:12)

If I were a woman, I should be very proud to own Mary of Bethany as my sister. She has been mentioned three times in the New Testament, and these Scriptures when placed together supply a most interesting progression of thought. It would seem that only Mary anticipated the death of her Master. While the other disciples dreamed of and hoped for the coming Kingdom, she looked into the Lord's eyes and read aright their grim purpose. Then, fearful lest she lost her opportunity, she gathered up her choicest treasure and gave it to Christ. She placed her flowers into His hand rather than upon His grave.

Mary Listening

The kitchen in the Bethany home was a very busy place. Jesus and His disciples were coming to lunch. Both Mary and Martha were thrilled at the prospect, in spite of the fact that much additional preparation would be necessary. When the party arrived, the sisters cordially welcomed them, and then Martha excused herself and hurried away to serve the meal. Alone, and with many jobs to do, she became increasingly flustered, and when she sought her sister's help, she discovered that Mary had followed Jesus into the parlour. Undoubtedly Martha tried hard, but eventually she opened the door and said, " Lord, dost thou not care that my sister hath left me to serve alone? bid her therefore that she come and help me " (Luke 10:40). Poor Martha! It was necessary to serve about twenty lunches that day, and only one pair of hands was available for the task. Then Jesus smiled, and gently replied, " Martha, Martha, thou art careful and troubled about many things: But one thing is needful, and Mary hath chosen that good part, that shall not be taken away from her." Martha was perfectly satisfied, and never complained again. The Lord Jesus loved a good listener, and Mary loved to listen.

Mary Learning

The scene has changed; the home at Bethany has become

a place filled with sorrow. The cruel hand of death has taken away the beloved brother; Lazarus has died. Then Mary heard of the approach of the Lord, and the events which followed His coming were rich in drama. The sorrowful sisters directed Christ to the tomb, and there witnessed His greatest manifestation of miraculous power. The Lord calmly looked at the place of shadows and said, " Lazarus, come forth," and to the surprise of all the crowd, " Lazarus came forth, bound hand and foot with graveclothes." Probably the sisters hardly remembered reaching their home that day. Wonder, excitement, joy, thrilled their entire beings; but later as they listened again to His gracious words, they became conscious of the gathering of even deeper shadows. The enraged Jews were bitter, because the new miracle had thrilled the crowds. Against the sombre background of their new plottings, the words of Jesus were easily remembered : " The Son of Man must be delivered into the hands of sinful men, and be crucified." Mary listened intently, and ultimately understood the meaning of His words.

Mary Loving

"Then Jesus six days before the passover came to Bethany," and at the request of Simon the leper, went with His friends to visit the convert's home. Probably Simon owed the greatest of all debts to Jesus. Somewhere out in the country, the Lord had touched and transformed him, and although the old name still clung to him, Simon was no longer a leper. In that simple home, Mary listened and learned again; and realizing that this was her final opportunity, she " took a pound of ointment of spikenard, very costly, and anointed the feet of Jesus, and wiped his feet with her hair : and the house was filled with the odour of the ointment " (John 12:3). The disciples were indignant at the apparent waste, but Jesus said, " Why trouble ye the woman? . . . in that she hath poured this ointment on my body, *she did it for my burial.*"

Well done, Mary! Some of us linger so long that our belated gifts can only beautify a tomb. You were in time. Congratulations!

A GRACIOUS WIFE . . . who believed in dreams

(MATTHEW 27:46)

The scene was set for the greatest drama in history. At the gates of the Governor's palace, an insistent mob clamoured for attention. The feast day was at hand, and before it commenced dirty work had to be done—and done quickly. As the sun arose to send its silvery beams across the darkened sky, the shouts of the people echoed along the cobbled streets. Awakened thus from his sleep, Pilate went forth to the trial of Jesus ignorant of the fact that his own soul would also be tried that day. Losing his balance on the slippery slope of indecision and compromise, the judge began to fall, and every passing hour brought him closer to disaster. How wonderful to recall that in those moments God sufficiently loved this sinner to plan a final attempt to save him. In common with all other aspects of redeeming love, this is beyond comprehension.

How Great was the Grace of God

Pilate's wife lay deep in slumber; she had not yet risen from her bed. Outside, her husband endeavoured to outwit the bigoted people who were beginning to blackmail him, and silently Christ stood listening. The woman stirred uneasily; she was restless. God had stooped to touch her slumbering eyes, and as she slept she dreamed— of Jesus. Suddenly, awaking with a start, she remembered that Pilate had gone to be the judge of the prophet.

Trembling with premonitions of disaster she wrote her urgent message, " Have thou nothing to do with that just man : for I have suffered many things this day in a dream because of him." If Pilate had taken her advice, his soul might have been saved. Had he not been so devoid of true understanding he would have recognized this dream to be a medium of grace. God never ceases His attempt at rescue while there is still a chance to succeed.

How Great was the Goodness of a Woman

Possibly the Governor dismissed this appeal as an intrusion into his own affairs. His wife should mind her own business. How could she understand the intricacies of this difficult case? These Jews had threatened to tell Cæsar, and if a charge of treason should be brought against him, his future would be ruined. He had nothing to lose in crucifying the prisoner; he had nothing to gain in resisting these arrogant Jews. Let her mind her own affairs! She did not understand. Ah, but she did. If misfortune overtook her husband, she could not escape; irrevocably her life was linked with his. She knew more. She knew that death was not the greatest of all tragedies. It was far better to die in honour than to live in shame. " Husband," she would have cried, " do that which is right. This man is just, therefore stand by him whatever the cost." Pilate should have been very proud of his noble partner. A good woman is the greatest jewel outside of heaven; a bad woman is the vilest creature outside of hell.

How Great was the Guilt of a Man

Rudely brushing aside both the grace of God and the entreaties of his gracious lady, Pilate washed his hands before the multitude, saying, " I am innocent of the blood of this just person." Then, in contradiction to his verdict, he sent Jesus forth to be scourged and crucified. He had washed his hands, but had never touched the soiled places of his soul. To save himself, he sacrificed his prisoner and his honour. Yet we are told that within seven years of his deed, a broken, destitute man removed from high office by the Governor of Syria, alone and unwanted by Cæsar, Pilate went out into the darkness of the night to hang himself. His body was found by a workman.

Poor, guilty man, I feel sorry for him. He met the Saviour and refused to love Him. And now it is dark—awfully dark.

JAIRUS . . . who probably broke all his vows

(MARK 5:22)

One of the strangest things in life is the way in which man is often made to do those things he had no intention of doing. Centuries ago Naaman in great rage vowed he would never wash in Jordan—but he did. Later, a burly fisherman said he would never deny his Lord—but he did. Probably the Christian Church often prayed for the persecutor Saul of Tarsus, and if the mad zealot heard of their intercessions, he too would have vowed never to bow before the Nazarene—but he did. And so it proved to be with Jairus. As the ruler of the synagogue his entire attitude would be antagonistic toward the new Teacher, and he would warn his people against attending His meetings. He himself was determined never to appeal to this enemy of Israel—but he did.

The Father's Desperation bringing him to Christ

Jairus was a ruler of the synagogue, and all matters of social and religious importance rested in his care. Proud of his ancestry, loving his faith, serving his God, and hating all heresy, he was a Hebrew of Hebrews. He lived in the nearby home, where for twelve wonderful years his charming little daughter had continually brightened his life. Dignity and love walked hand in hand through the life of this favoured man; but when his daughter became critically ill, the thought of her preservation swept all else aside. When Jairus heard of Jesus, immediately his heart became a battle-ground where love and pride fought a battle to the death. Love suggested an appeal to the great Physician; pride reminded of the warnings which in all probability had been given weekly to the congregation. "And, behold, there cometh one of the rulers of the synagogue, Jairus by name; and when he saw Jesus, he fell at His feet." How helpless—how humble—how hopeful; these were the three stages through which the soul of this man fought its way to victory.

The Friend's Doubt blinding him to Christ

"And Jesus went with him; and much people followed Him, and thronged Him. And a certain woman, which had an issue of blood twelve years . . . came in the press behind, and touched His garment." The healing of the woman occasioned a little delay, and to the anxious father this was tragic. "Then came there from the ruler of the synagogue's house certain which said, Thy daughter is dead: why troublest thou the Master any further?" These words were probably spoken in sincerity, but were most damaging to the hopes of the desperate man. The people said, "The case is now past hope. If only Christ had come earlier, something might have been done. Come home, therefore, and arrange for the funeral." There are still many people who seem strangely related to these friends of a bygone age. They limit the power of God, and believe that beyond certain obscure limits every case becomes hopeless. Their unbelief says, "Trouble not the Master any further."

The Fool's Disdain banishing him from Christ

"As soon as Jesus heard the word that was spoken, He saith unto the ruler of the synagogue, Be not afraid, only believe . . . and when He was come in, He saith unto them, Why make ye this ado, and weep? the damsel is not dead, but sleepeth. And they laughed Him to scorn." And never was laughter so ill-timed as in that stricken home. Possibly the people were angry because their leader had betrayed the cause of Israel—he had gone to solicit help from the accursed Carpenter. They looked at the grieving ruler and scornfully chuckled at the apparent stupidity of Christ's statement. Their foolishness robbed them of an inestimable privilege. Christ put them all out, and closed the door. Such blatant, arrogant sin could never be permitted to linger in His presence, either here or in eternity. Should He ever deem it necessary to close an eternal door, the consequences would be most grave for those left on the outside. "He taketh the father and the mother of the damsel, and them that were with Him, and entereth in where the damsel was lying. And He took the damsel by the hand." His whispered words were as the balm of Gilead to wounded souls. Slowly the colour came back to the ashen cheeks of the girl; slowly two sleepy eyes opened, and in the following moments peace returned to the sorrowful parents. Yes, Jairus probably broke all his earlier vows when he came to Christ; but it was better to do that then, than to break his heart for ever.

THE MAN OF BETHSAIDA . . . who needed
a second touch

Chorazin, Bethsaida, and Capernaum were towns situated very near to the north-eastern corner of the sea of Galilee, and were probably the first places to feel the impact of the preaching of John Baptist. Their citizens were among the first to hear the fiery message of the wilderness orator; but during the following months a startling change took place in their midst. They saw in the coming of the revival crowds the opportunity of increasing their wealth, and gradually their business instincts overcame the desire for spiritual health. The coming of Jesus increased these possibilities, and it was not a cause for amazement when Christ uttered His message of condemnation. He said, "Woe unto thee, Chorazin! woe unto thee, Bethsaida! for if the mighty works which have been done in you, had been done in Tyre and Sidon, they would have repented long ago in sackcloth and ashes. . . . And thou, Capernaum, which art exalted unto heaven, shall be brought down to hell" (Matt. 11:21-23).

How Serious can be His Anger

Every student of the Pauline epistles knows that the first chapter of the letter to the Romans talks of people whose villainy made God give them up. It would appear that Bethsaida and her sister cities had likewise become irretrievably lost. "And He cometh to Bethsaida; and they bring a blind man unto Him, and besought Him to touch him. And Jesus took the blind man by the hand, *and led him out of the town.*" And after the Saviour had performed the great miracle, He "sent him away to his house, saying, *Neither go into the town, nor tell it to any in the town.*" We may consider two interpretations of this command. Knowing the evil tendencies of the townspeople, the Lord may have warned His convert against possible persecution. Yet, on the other hand, it seems that He deliberately deprived the people of an opportunity to hear the glad tidings. They had witnessed miracles already, and would only sneer at the man's testimony. When Christ refrains from sending His message to a man or a community, that moment marks the end of spiritual opportunity.

How Sincere can be His Love

" And He took the blind man by the hand, and led him out of the town; and when He had spit on his eyes, and put His hands upon him, He asked him if he saw ought. And he looked up and said, I see men as trees, walking. After that He put his hands again upon his eyes, and made him look up, and he was restored, and saw every man clearly." The Lord Jesus did not command a disciple to lead the blind man; He preferred to do so Himself, and personally superintended every part of the process of healing. Many teachers have wondered why Christ did not restore the man's sight immediately. Perhaps He realized that the sudden inrush of brilliant daylight would have occasioned more harm than good, and His omniscience ordained that the transformation should take place gradually. Yet, whatever the reason, many Christians are glad it happened thus, for Christ's methods indicate that all experiences are not alike. Some saints can proudly point to the actual moment of their conversion; others cannot, for in their case sight came gradually. Surely the pre-eminent thing is that we are able to see, and not the way in which our eyes were opened. Would it not have been stupid if the man of Bethsaida had met Bartimæus and had argued with him that his eyesight was unorthodox because he had not seen men as trees walking!

How Strong can be His Power

" After that He put His hands again upon his eyes." The Lord Jesus never leaves a task half-finished. Graciously He watches His people, and when it becomes necessary to place His hand upon the needy, He is able to do it. No case is too difficult, for His power is unlimited. It would seem that He brought a second blessing to His convert from Bethsaida. Yet there is a greater blessing awaiting the children of God. It comes when we take Christ's hand and refuse to let it go. Then there is no need for a second blessing, for we live in the constant enjoyment of one unending experience of companionship. Then moment by moment He imparts to us of His own fullness, and together we walk through time into eternity, to remain with Him for ever.

BARTIMAEUS . . . who could see with his eyes shut

Vision is a bewildering thing, and one sometimes has difficulty in understanding the various ramifications of a man's sight. Some people with excellent eyes succeed in seeing nothing. Others who are blind succeed in watching a world. Queer, but true! Many things can hinder vision. A cataract, a fog, a piece of dirt, or even a dizzy faint can plunge a man into blackness. This is not surprising; but when a blind man can succeed in identifying objects, and recognizing at a distance what others cannot see close at hand, ordinary explanations seem inadequate. Blind Bartimæus excelled in these qualities. He could see with his eyes shut.

He Saw that His Greatest Opportunity had Come

" And they came to Jericho: and as He went out of Jericho with His disciples and a great number of people, blind Bartimæus, the son of Timæus, sat by the wayside begging. And when he heard that it was Jesus of Nazareth, he began to cry out, and say, Jesus, thou son of David, have mercy on me." Suddenly his philosophy of life underwent its greatest change. He had previously known but one item of interest, and that was how to increase his earnings—he was a beggar. A crowd always brightened his prospects, for his coins generally increased with the number of passers-by. Yet when the many people began to crowd around, he lost all interest in monetary gains and thought only of the nearness of Jesus. The great Healer was in the vicinity, and that meant the approach of opportunity for a poor, blind man. Throwing caution to the winds, Bartimæus began to cry out for help.

He Saw that this Opportunity could Easily Pass By

His inward vision increased moment by moment, and realizing that he had no time to lose, he appealed loudly to the Saviour. He was very wise, for Christ was on His way *out of Jericho.* Had he waited another minute, the Master would have been out of earshot, and he would have missed his great chance. Again his voice echoed above the heads of the people, and finally some of the crowd told him to be quiet. The beggar listened to their advice and immediately rejected it, for he had already realized that his eyesight would be of more value to him than the plaudits of men. Their coins might reward his obedience, but they could never lighten his darkness. "Jesus, thou son of David," he cried again and again. Desperately he lifted his voice, determined not to lose his great chance of gaining eyesight.

He Saw that the Opportunity Might Never Return

And he was right! The Lord Jesus was on His way to Jerusalem, to die for the sins of a world. Never again would He itinerate through the country, making known the glad tidings of the Gospel; for "His hour had come," and He had steadfastly set His face toward the cross. That was His final visit to Jericho, and if the beggar had lost his opportunity, he would have remained in the dark for the rest of his life. It is never safe to postpone to a later date something that demands urgent attention. Bartimæus knew it was a case of "now or never," and refused to be silenced by the critical crowd. For a blind man, his eyesight was very good indeed!

He Saw that Christ's Way was Better than his Own

"And Jesus stood still, and commanded him to be called. And they called the blind man, saying unto him, Be of good comfort, rise; He calleth thee. And he, casting away his garment, rose, and came to Jesus. . . . And Jesus said unto him, Go thy way, thy faith hath made thee whole. And immediately he received his sight, and followed Jesus in the way" (Mark 10:49-52). The gift of eyesight included many other blessings, and at the earliest moment Bartimæus would want to see his family. Perhaps the Lord had this in mind when He said "Go thy way," but the beggar looked into the face of Jesus and forgot all else. He had no desire to go anywhere except after his Lord, and " as he followed Christ in the way " his soul-hunger was satisfied in fellowship with the Saviour. Yet he recognized this fact even before he experienced it. He could see with his eyes shut! Can we?

THE PARENTS OF JESUS . . . and the greatest of Bible problems
(LUKE 2:44)

There are many problems in the Scriptures, but most of them can be solved by serious thought. The intricacies of theology are apt to simplify when concentrated study can be brought to bear upon the text. Here, however, is a problem beyond my explanation. It baffles me because it is contrary to humanity. It is the account of two parents who lost their little boy. I don't understand it.

DISCOVERY 1. *They had lost Jesus*

The feast had just ended, and every road leading from the holy city was thronged with travellers. Friends laughed and chatted, business men seized the opportunity for selling goods; and while jocularly they jostled and pushed each other, here and there a smiling man endeavoured to manœuvre his way through the milling throng. They had all had a grand time, and hoped it would not be too long before they returned once again. Mary and Joseph belonged to the party from Nazareth, and as the sun climbed the sky they went under the old archway, through the gate, and the journey had begun. " And the child Jesus tarried behind in Jerusalem; and Joseph and His mother knew not of it. But they, *supposing Him to have been in the company,* went a day's journey; and they sought Him among their kinsfolk and acquaintance." Somehow I have never been able to visualize my mother returning from any holiday and going a day's journey without seeing me. It matters not how far that journey had taken the parents of Jesus, the fact remains they had breakfast, lunch, and possibly a late afternoon meal, and never once had they seen His face. They had not lost their love for Him; they had not lost their faith; *they had lost Him.* The greatest help in trying to understand the story comes in remembering that often we also lose Him as we journey along the road of life. We have boundless faith, but we go long distances without seeing His face. It is always a silly thing to do.

DISCOVERY 2. *It was their own fault*

This was very hard to admit; and even when He had

been restored to them, His mother asked, " Son, why hast *thou* thus dealt with us?" She might have said, " Son, we are sorry we went without you." They had lost Him because they had been too interested in the material things of life. The feast, the services, the temple, the crowds, and the fellowship, had completely banished all other thoughts from their minds. Their boy had been forgotten and neglected. There was no sin in thinking of those soul-thrilling experiences, but first things in life should always occupy first place. When something comes between the Saviour and the soul, that something immediately becomes sin. I dare not go one step without Christ's aid. It is among the greatest tragedies in life that so many people find it possible to journey on and on without even thinking of God. Men become so absorbed in business and sport and other pursuits, that they forget the claims of Christ and journey on without Him. It is always a very unwise action, and leads to disappointment and regret.

DISCOVERY 3. *They found Him where they least expected Him to be*

" And it came to pass, that after three days they found Him in the temple, sitting in the midst of the doctors, both hearing them, and asking them questions. And all that heard him were astonished at his understanding and answers." *After three days.* This is a most interesting item of information, and it appears that they only sought Him in the temple when they had already finished their seeking elsewhere. Probably they had visited all the likely places in the city; yet, although they searched every street, their efforts had been in vain, and each night they despaired and wondered where He could be. Finally, as a last resort they came into the temple, and behold, He was there speaking with the leaders of the nation. Had they gone first into the temple, they would have saved themselves a great deal of trouble and heartache. Let us remember that Christ can always be found close to the altar of God. If we find Him there, He will be ready to walk with us on the road to our home.

THE GREAT LEADERS . . . who missed God's blessing

(LUKE 5:17)

"And it came to pass on a certain day, as He was teaching, that there were Pharisees and doctors of the law sitting by, which were come out of every town of Galilee, and Judea, and Jerusalem: and the power of the Lord was present to heal them." This verse suggests certain questions. (i) What attraction brought together this select company of religious dignitaries from every town in the country? Why did these celebrated people converge on one central spot? I have often thought of our denominational assemblies, to which all the churches send their representatives. I have wondered if something of the sort were being held in this town, and if these ministers, far from their congregations, seized the opportunity of hearing the new Teacher—a privilege they would have shunned nearer home? (ii) Why did God specially prepare for the coming of these men—the power of the Lord was present to heal *them*? (iii) What hindrances prevented the receiving of the blessing?

A Personal Need

Somewhere in the district, the Lord Jesus addressed His audience; and it must have been a wonderful meeting. The building was packed to its utmost capacity, and it is not too much to suggest that the special visitors arrived early. A late-comer found it necessary to enter through the ceiling! They claimed their seats and waited for the sermon. It would be most interesting to know their reactions to His message. Ignorant of the fact that God had planned to draw near to them, they listened critically and went away unblessed. (i) Were they too blind to recognize their own need? Were they watching others, and not considering that they might have been His first converts? (ii) Even if they knew their need, were they too proud to admit it? Did the dignity of the synagogue forbid bowing before a Carpenter? (iii) Did the fear of men hold them back? Were they conscious of the presence of colleagues, and were they mindful of the repercussions that would follow any rash action? These questions are so interesting because all these types still exist.

A Personal Appeal

The story provides a glorious contrast. Elsewhere in the district a man lay at home sick of the palsy. He was desperately anxious to meet Jesus of Nazareth, but had no means of transport until four friends volunteered to carry him to the meeting. (i) Unlike the priests, he already knew his own personal need of Christ. His case had baffled other healers. (ii) He was not too proud for his fellowmen to know of his desire, for he chose to enter the service in such a novel fashion that the world has never ceased talking about him. (iii) He also knew that his actions would lead to expensive repercussions. He was damaging the property of some other man—a man who in all probability would have much to say concerning it. In blissful abandon the sufferer urged his friends to lift the tiles. Perhaps even God smiled as He watched from heaven.

A Personal Saviour

This man had obviously determined to meet Christ. He intended to present his own petition whatever the cost. The Lord Jesus ceased preaching as the plaster commenced to fall. It would have been futile to speak while the audience stared upward at an ever-increasing hole in the ceiling. " And when He saw their faith, He said unto the sick of the palsy, Man, thy sins are forgiven thee. And the scribes and the Pharisees began to reason, saying, Who is this that speaketh blasphemies? Who can forgive sins, but God alone?" Thus their Bethel became a debating chamber. The power of God was present to heal them— and not one was healed. I do not know if the convert was ever required to pay damages; nor do I know what hard words might have been spoken to him. Yet however great his account, it never equalled the other account settled when Christ said "Thy sins are forgiven thee." How sad is the thought—a man may only be a step from the Kingdom, and yet miss it by a mile!

THE SINFUL WOMAN ... whose silent confession echoes through a world (LUKE 7:37)

How can a man obtain the forgiveness of his sin? There have been numerous answers to this important question. It has been suggested that man must endeavour by his own merit to increase his credit account in the bank of heaven. It has also been taught that the granting of forgiveness is the prerogative of certain ecclesiastical leaders; that one must conform to particular Church laws in order to obtain the coveted treasure. Other people prefer to seek their answer within the message of Holy Scripture.

A Woman's Conviction

Somewhere within the shadowy hovels of an eastern city, a poor woman prepared for her nightly escapade. She was a great sinner, and regularly went out to break the heart of God. We do not know what ugly combination of circumstances had brought her to such low levels of morality; nor do we know whether or not she cared. She took from its resting place her box of perfume, and appreciating its powers of attraction, she used it to adorn her person. Then, extinguishing the lamp, she slipped into the darkness, and her night had begun. Somewhere she probably saw a crowd, and hearing the voice of a Stranger, she drew near and came face to face with Jesus. We can only guess as to the nature of His message, but we are sure His words reached her soul. Soon she forgot the purpose of her coming into the city, and retraced her steps homeward. She had met Jesus, and His words could never be forgotten. She felt unclean; she hardly knew what to do; she loathed herself. Thus she took the first step along the pathway to pardon.

A Woman's Contrition

Mechanically she lifted her precious box of ointment, and as her fingers closed around the treasure, she realized she was about to make her greatest decision. If she accepted and followed the Teacher's way of life, she would never again need this questionable adornment. The purpose for which it was meant would be non-existent in her life. Should she take it to Him? How would she earn her living? How would she obtain bread? She did not know. It was sufficient to know that she needed cleansing, and that never again would she grieve her God. She made inquiries at the meeting place, and ascertaining that Jesus had gone to dine with Simon the Pharisee, she followed to the well-known home. " And behold, a woman of the city, which was a sinner, when she knew that Jesus sat at meat in the Pharisee's house, brought an alabaster box of ointment, and stood at His feet behind Him weeping, and began to wash His feet with tears, and did wipe them with the hairs of her head." Her conviction had deepened to contrition. We must not confuse these two steps. Conviction reveals man's sinfulness; contrition reveals man's sorrow for sin. Many people have known conviction of soul, yet have persistently pursued their path of evil. ·Contrition is much nearer to God's heart than conviction.

A Woman's Confession

" She anointed His feet with the ointment." Bowing before the mounting storm of criticism, she listened to the words of the Lord, and found peace. He alone read aright the confession behind the broken box. He knew that she was trying to say, " Lord, I shall never need this again, for the old life is now dead." " And He said unto her, Thy sins are forgiven . . . Thy faith hath saved thee; go in peace." And while the onlookers saw just a broken box, He saw a broken heart and tenderly healed it. The perfume of that box of ointment slowly filled the room, and then escaped to fill the world; it is still with us. We imagine the woman's home-going; and if sleep seemed elusive that night, maybe she still thought of His words, " Thy sins are forgiven . . . go in peace." She was not commanded to reach new heights of morality in order to atone for former failures; nor was she instructed to bow before the priest in the synagogue. The only confessional box she ever knew was the small one broken in His presence. How can a man obtain the forgiveness of sins? He must realize his need; he should be ashamed of his guilt; and in sincerity of soul he should seek the Saviour. " None who to Jesus came were ever turned away."

THE GADARENES . . . who preferred swine
to the Saviour (Luke 8:37)

He was mad and completely terrifying, and no one ever approached his home among the tombs. His long, untidy hair reached to his massive shoulders; his eyes, furtive and restless, were alternately light with excitement and dark with depression; and his only pleasure—if pleasure we might call it—came when he was near the dead. The desolation of his surroundings matched that of his heart. He was a haunted, hunted man, the mention of whose name made the citizens tremble. They said he was possessed of devils. And then the Lord Jesus came. . . .

The Peace

When the Master appeared over the brow of the hill, the demented captive stared; something snapped in his brain, and with a wild, vehement cry he rushed toward the invader. Unperturbed, the Lord awaited the onrushing maniac, and suddenly a surprising thing took place. The watching disciples hardly knew how it happened, for in some strange, mysterious fashion the running man hesitated, and fell at the feet of their Master. When the prostrate man lifted his head, the dawn of a new day was beginning to shine in his eyes. Christ had challenged and conquered the indwelling demons; the power of sin had been broken, and into the liberated soul poured the boundless peace of God. How wonderful it is to remember that this Christ is the same yesterday, and to-day, and for ever. The greatest evidence for Christ and the Gospel is not in the multiplicity of churches, but rather that His word can still break the power of sin.

The Price

In a little while the people came out to see what had been done, and there at the feet of his deliverer they found the demoniac, " clothed, and in his right mind; *and they were afraid*." One might ask, of what were they afraid? Surely this wonderful day should be recognized as the most outstanding in the history of their seaside homes? They looked at the gently moving waters of the lake, and shuddered as they recalled how two thousand swine had

111

disappeared beneath the waves. This much-to-be-desired miracle had been most expensive. A single deliverance had cost a fortune. One of their comrades had suffered irretrievable loss, and if Jesus of Nazareth continued His mission of healing, other farmers would soon be joining him in the ranks of poverty. They looked at Jesus, "and besought Him to depart." Are there not others to-day who act similarly?

The Poverty

That day, as far as we are able to tell from the record, they lost a priceless opportunity. When the tiny craft sailed out over the lake, it carried far more than men. No one can be absolutely certain, but this at least can be said: that there is no reference to any later visit made by Christ. Possibly He never returned, and we shall never know just how many miracles might have been performed among those people if they had not preferred swine.

> Rabbi, begone. Thy powers
> Bring loss to us and ours.
> Our ways are not thine:
> Thou lovest men; we—swine.
>
> Oh, get thee hence, Omnipotence,
> And take this fool of thine;
> His soul, what care we for his soul?
> What good to us that thou hast made him whole,
> Since we have lost our swine?
>
> And Christ went sadly.
> He had wrought for them a sign
> Of love, and hope, and tenderness divine:
> They wanted swine.
>
> Christ stands without your door,
>   and gently knocks;
> But if your gold or swine
>   the entrance blocks,
> He forces no man's hold; he will depart
> And leave you to the pleasures of your heart.

And so this Stranger comes to us. Sometimes in the most unexpected of ways, and often unannounced, He draws near. Let us be sure that He never comes empty-handed. Should His coming mean sacrifice, we shall do well to consider that ultimately "no good thing will be withheld from them who walk uprightly."

JOHN BAPTIST . . . and a study in shaking reeds (Luke 7:24)

There are two interpretations of John Baptist's question, "Art thou He that should come, or look we for another?" Some declare that after his eighteen months' imprisonment, his faith was beginning to waver, and that his doubts found expression in this question. He had become a reed shaken by the wind. The Bible has much to say of the winds that shake souls.

The Wind of Adversity

If this interpretation be correct, John's faith and courage had been undermined by the things he had endured. Amid the soul-thrilling excitement of the Jordan meetings, he had cried, "Behold the Lamb of God, which taketh away the sins of the world." During those memorable meetings he had been a light to a darkened nation; but now, so it is suggested, he had slipped into the shadows. Adversity is a cold, wintry blast, and only men with a superabundance of backbone can resist the temptation to lean away from it. Then blue skies of vision are apt to be overcast; inspiring songs of victorious faith are apt to be hushed, and amid the perplexities of current events the soul pauses to ask, Why has God permitted this to happen? Did I make a mistake in trusting Christ? "Art thou he that should come, or look we for another?"

The Wind of Hypocrisy

Our example comes from Old Testament literature. We are told in 1 Samuel 2:12-17 that the sins of Eli's sons had become very great before the Lord and before Israel. Their disgusting behaviour had made the people "abhor the offering of God." It is surely not difficult to understand the outworkings of such dislike. Recognizing the hypocrisy of the priests, men turned from the house of God, and abstained from fulfilling His laws. Much might be said on their behalf, but the fact remains that they had looked too long at hypocrites and correspondingly had lost their vision of God. The strong wind of hypocrisy had proved them to be reeds. They permitted poor, disappointing priests to spoil the service of the sanctuary. And are not their type still with us? Are there not multitudes of people who cry about the presence of hypocrites in the churches, and do they not offer this as an excuse for their own non-attendance at the sanctuary? Alas, they are reeds shaken by the wind.

The Wind of Worldliness

There is something supremely pathetic about Paul's last message to Timothy: " Do thy diligence to come shortly unto me: for Demas hath forsaken me, having loved this present world, and is departed unto Thessalonica." How sad it is to relate that he who had been Paul's companion in the work of evangelizing failed to stay at his post. He had weathered many storms, but suddenly he allowed his eyes to linger upon the charming enjoyments of sin. He went away in search of carnal pleasures. " He loved this present world." Let us feel profoundly sorry for Demas. The cross would have ruined his taste for worldly pleasure; and worldliness would have come between him and the cross. He would be in no man's land, friendless and alone. Poor Demas! He had proved to be a reed shaken by the wind. He lacked the stiffening effect of a good backbone, and bowed at the wrong altar.

Was John the Baptist a man of this type? Surely not. Did not Christ look at the crowd and say, " What went ye out into the wilderness for to see? A reed shaken with the wind? But what went ye out for to see? A man clothed in soft raiment? . . . What went ye out for to see? A prophet? Yea, and much more than a prophet. . . . Among those that are born of women there is not a greater prophet than John the Baptist." John was not a shaking reed. He had listened to the complaints of his disciples, and realized that Christ alone could solve their problems. He was too wise to argue with them. He probably smiled and said, " Go and ask the Master, and tell Him that I sent you."

Well done, John. You came to point men to Christ, and you did it to the end.

THE RICH MAN . . . a drama in three acts

(LUKE 12:16)

Act One

He was a splendid young man, and the villagers loved him. He was a ruler, but he was also a brother beloved; he had kept the commandments from his childhood days. His happiness must have been complete until Jesus came preaching in the little village. The ruler had never heard a preacher like this Stranger, upon whose countenance shone the light of heaven, whose words had the ring of authority, and whose charm none could deny. It was not a cause for amazement when later he came running to ask, " Good Master, what must I do to inherit eternal life?" Jesus answered, "If thou wilt enter into life, keep the commandments." " But Master, all these have I kept from my youth up. What lack I yet?" Gravely the Teacher listened. This was a nice young man; so honest and so sincere. Eagerly the ruler awaited an answer, and had he been able to thought-read, he probably would have read, " Well done. You have indeed made a great discovery. Keeping the commandments will never bring eternal life. Others will talk of their deeds and will measure themselves by the standards of earthly virtue, not knowing that their best righteousness is to God as filthy rags." Then Jesus said, "If thou wilt be perfect, go and sell that thou hast, and give to the poor, and thou shalt have treasure in heaven: *and come and follow me.*" But when the young man heard that saying, he went away sorrowful: for he had great possessions. Did he ever reappear in the Gospel story?

Act Two

The farmhouse stood silently in the countryside, and from its chimneys the thin wisps of smoke lazily climbed into transparency. A wealthy man leaned on his gate and intently gazed at his crops. They were wonderful this year. Indeed, he had seldom seen such a harvest; it was obvious that his barns would be unable to store his possessions. What could he do? To give to the poor would be bad business. Let them work for their food. He would build larger barns, and then take his ease. His problem was settled. He smiled. He went to bed thinking about the new project, and wakened up in eternity. A voice had whispered in the stillness of the night, saying, " Thou fool, this night thy soul shall be required of thee." " What shall I do? " asked the rich young ruler. " What shall I do? " asked the older man. They spoke the same language —*were they the same man?* Of course, no one can be dogmatic about this, and it does not really matter. There is truth here if we seek it. The rich pauper was buried, but the question arises once again—Did he ever reappear on the Gospel page?

Act Three

Some time later the Lord Jesus said, " The rich man also died, and was buried; And in hell he lift up his eyes, being in torments." When we read the account in Luke 16, it becomes increasingly clear that once again the question in eternity was, " What shall I do? " There seems to be a continuity of thought in these three stories. The characters may not have been identical, nevertheless here is experience indeed. It is an established fact that the over-whelming majority of Christians are won before they reach the age of twenty. Once a young man has passed this age, the possibility is that soon he will be engrossed in business, and most of his interests will be earthly. Many a successful business man who has no time for God remembers the youthful days when his interests were loftier and holier. Alas, at the end of such a life is eternal frustration and boundless sorrow. Perhaps it was this fact which inspired the wise man to say, " Remember now thy creator in the days of thy youth, while the evil days come not, nor the years draw nigh when thou shalt say I have no pleasure in them." Yesterday has gone for ever. To-morrow I may be gone, also—but where? Here is food for thought.

THE PRODIGAL . . . who went to school in a pigsty (Luke 15:15-17)

God always says the best possible about a man, and in that respect His account of the prodigal son is somewhat different from the many sermons preached in the pulpit. The preacher invariably speaks about the sin of the selfish boy who revelled in the lustful enjoyments of the far country. This is considered to be a great message for tramps and drunkards. Yet in His approach to the theme, God says that the real man was not responsible for the crimes of the prodigal. These were brought about through the cruel activities of a deplorable understudy.

The Real Man Submerged

Yes, it is a thrilling thought that God always seeks the best in a man. He knew the prodigal would soon come to himself. Surging passions and tumultuous emotions had temporarily swamped the real man. Studdart Kennedy often said,

> There's summat that pulls us up,
> And summat that pulls us down;
> And the consequence is that we wobble
> Twixt muck and a golden crown.

Here is a story of moments when the downward pull seemed the greater of the two. Thus a man had been ruined. He appeared to be utterly vile; but let us be patient—the real man will yet lift up his head.

The Real Man Surviving

When we study the awful moral and spiritual depravity of the prodigal, it appears difficult to find virtue in his character. "He spent all his substance in riotous living," and sank to depths where no decent citizen would help him. His entire background seems sordid and immoral, yet underneath his recklessness lay the soul of a real man. Someone has said,

> There's so much bad in the best of us,
> And so much good in the worst of us,
> It ill behoves any one of us
> To find fault with the rest of us.

We therefore do well if we consider three vital facts. (i) *God's Vision.* He saw that the real man still existed. (ii) *God's Faith.* He believed the real man would ultimately triumph. (iii) *God's Patience.* He was willing to wait until such a miracle became possible.

The Real Man Suggesting

Sometimes pigs can be splendid schoolmasters. They are expert tutors of the fact that they who never look up generally live in squalor and end in tragedy. The prodigal listened to their grunts and learned to appreciate the music of his home. "And when he came to himself." An identical expression is used to describe the trance or sleep-walking of Peter when by divine intervention he was brought out of prison (Acts 12:11). Outside in the city street he came to himself and realized that he had been a man doing and saying things for which he was not quite intellectually responsible. The phase had passed, and the sleepiness had vanished from his eyes. In like manner the prodigal awakened and realized—(i) *His need for penitence.* "Father, I have sinned before heaven." (ii) *His need for prayer.* "Make me as one of thy hired servants." (iii) *His need to proceed immediately,* or his finest resolutions would be useless.

The Real Man Supreme

Once again we may profitably consider three things. (i) *How great was his sincerity.* "Father, I have sinned against heaven and in thy sight, and am no more worthy to be called thy son." He realized that his greater sin was against God; the sin against his father was secondary. (ii) *How great was his salvation.* "But the father said to his servants, Bring forth the best robe . . . For this my son was dead, and is alive again; he was lost, and is found." (iii) *How great was his service.* This would provide a strange contrast to the half-hearted service which he rendered before he left his home. This time it would be born of gratitude. His heart would strengthen his hands.

Surely the Lord Jesus loved to tell this story, for He believed the real man existed in every fallen soul. To seek such men He left His throne in glory and came down to die on a cross. He is supremely thrilled each time a prodigal turns his face homeward.

ZACCHAEUS ... the dwarf who became a giant
(LUKE 19:3)

This is a simple study in height. There are very tall men who are unable to look over a small disappointment; there are tiny Davids who can look over the shoulder of Goliath to see God. This incident happened at the close of the Saviour's ministry, when His fame had been spread abroad; when everyone in the land would have heard of the great Carpenter. His amazing miracles could not have passed unnoticed. Yet suddenly, as though he had come from overseas, we find a man who knew nothing about Jesus. " And behold, there came a man named Zacchæus, which was the chief among the publicans, and he was rich. And he sought to see Jesus *who he was.*"

Zacchæus the Dwarf

We cannot possibly avoid a question. Where had this man been during the three memorable years of the Saviour's ministry? It appears that he had had no contact with the Lord. He had not even seen Him. Such a condition hardly seems possible. At best we can only hazard a guess, but it is significant that this man was chief among the publicans. He had not only sold his services to the accursed Romans, he had attained to some official importance in the esteem of his employers. His duty was to stimulate the wavering tax-gatherers, and see that they never faltered in the odious task of collecting money from the unwilling taxpayers. He would be especially detested and isolated by his fellow-countrymen. His friends would be few, and his social activities unimportant. He avoided Jewish feasts, and shunned crowds where his presence would lead to embarrassment. Thus the ministry of Jesus had never been able to reach him. Poor Zacchæus was so small that his vision was limited to Jewry. He probably hated them.

Zacchæus the Desirous

After three years a most interesting thing occurred. One day he sallied forth into the street and became aware of a great crowd. Naturally he wondered why so many people had gathered. When he was told about the coming of the

Prophet, for once in a while he ceased allowing Jewry to fill his horizons. He, the chief of the publicans, became so anxious to see the visiting Teacher that he looked round for a vantage point; for he was little of stature. Within a few moments he was safely seated in the branches of a tree, and the stage was set for his most thrilling experience. As long as he thought of Jews, he could only see Jews. Once he commenced growing, wonderful things immediately became possible. After all, *there was a Christ* somewhere. Yet many people still find difficulty in believing this fact. They can only watch hypocrites. Yes, this is definitely a study in height.

Zacchæus the Discoverer

Amazed and curiously interested, he watched as the Stranger came along the cobbled street. Then suddenly the Teacher came across to say, " Zacchæus, make haste and come down; for to-day I must abide at thy house." And Zacchæus came down, and received Him joyfully. Instantly it seemed as if the little dwarf had explored unlimited continents. He realized that he was known by name to Jesus. He discovered, too, that Christ had come seeking for sinners, even the chief of the publicans. He became aware that whether he liked it or not, he had to make a choice; that Christ was waiting for his response— a response that could only mean a whole-hearted welcome into the place called home. Then he discovered how little men can suddenly grow tall. He had climbed a tree because he was small; he came down because he had grown. All men are apt to increase their stature when they respond to Christ. And from that day forward the little-big man ceased looking at people. His eyes were focused on the Master. " And Zacchæus stood, and said unto the Lord; Behold, Lord, the half of my goods I give to the poor; and if I have taken anything from any man by false accusation, I restore him fourfold. And Jesus said unto him, This day is salvation come to this house . . . For the Son of man is come to seek and to save that which was lost." God desires that all men should see Christ. Sometimes He even plants trees—but man must decide to climb!

SIMON PETER . . . who sat at two fires

During the night in which our Lord was betrayed, two men passed through a doorway into the darkness of the city. One man turned and walked into the bitterness of eternal remorse; the other walked into the arms of God. At that doorway Judas and Simon Peter parted for ever. The Lord has set forth in detail the account of Peter's great tragedy, and since his path of sorrow is so clearly defined, let us consider it.

The Downward Path to Calamity

Peter should have known better, for the Lord had said unto him, "Simon, Simon, behold, Satan hath desired to have you, that he may sift you as wheat " ; but in self-confidence the disciple replied, " Lord, I am ready to go with thee, both into prison, and to death." Almost immediately he began to drift from Christ. (i) *And Peter followed afar off.* This was his first mistake. When a Christian begins to backslide, the commencement of the trouble can always be traced to this cause. The loss of intimate communion leads to disaster. (ii) *And Peter warmed himself at the fire* (Mark 14:67). This was his second mistake. Following in the distance, he grew cold and was attracted to the fire—the enemies' fire. There appeared to be little harm in his actions, but real danger lurked in the company gathered there. And this story is very true to present-day life. When a Christian becomes cold in his heart, the fires of worldliness will always provide a source of attraction. It is a time of supreme danger. (iii) *And Peter sat down among them* (Luke 22:55). Any plan concerning an early departure was forgotten. He intended to stay and enjoy fellowship around the fire. This was his greatest mistake. Something was certainly wrong when a disciple of Christ felt at ease among the Master's enemies. (iv) *And Peter denied his Lord—" I know Him not."* We are told that Simon Peter denied thrice, yet strange to relate, the denials were not identical. The first denial concerned his allegiance to Christ. It is always thus. (v) *And Peter denied his association with the disciples—the Church.* To the accusation, " Thou art also of *them*," he replied, " Man,

I am not." Satan is never content with a first denial. He will endeavour to bring the backslider away from the fellowship of the saints, for otherwise the man may recover. (vi) And Peter began to curse and swear (Mark 14:71). When he was accused of speaking with a different dialect, he used their type of expression and so overcame their final objections. His sin appeared to sever all his connections with Christ, and he seemed completely lost. He stumbled through the doorway into the darkness of the street, *but took the right turn.*

The Upward Path to Christ

" And the Lord turned and looked upon Peter, and Peter remembered the word of the Lord . . . and he went out and wept bitterly." Somewhere in the city he broke his heart. (i) *The risen Lord sent a special invitation asking Peter to return.* When Mary came to the tomb she was met by an angel who said, " Go your way, tell His disciples *and Peter* that He goeth before you into Galilee: there shall ye see Him, as He said " (Mark 16:7). We must remember that in spite of his great mistakes, Peter was still a disciple. Special mention was made of his name, for this was a great effort to bring back a wanderer. (ii) *The risen Lord personally sought for Simon.* When the Emmaus travellers returned to announce the resurrection of Christ, they heard the disciples saying, " The Lord is risen indeed, *and hath appeared unto Simon.*" Paul also cited this great appearance, for obviously it was known to all the Church (1 Cor. 15:5). The Lord probably knew of Peter's shame and reluctance to accept the invitation, and therefore went forth in search of him. What they said to each other has remained a great secret. It is better that way. (iii) *The Lord publicly gave a new commission to his restored follower.* The scene which took place at the edge of the sea of Galilee has now become famous. At another fire Peter made his threefold confession and received his thrilling commission. His service on the day of Pentecost, and throughout the following years, demonstrated how complete had been his recovery. We are able to understand why he wrote, " Unto you therefore which believe, He is precious " (1 Peter 2:7).

SIMON THE CYRENIAN . . . the most privileged man in the world (LUKE 23:26)

The entire Gospel story may be described as an account of God's giving to men. At Bethlehem He gave His Son to the world; in the ministry of Jesus He gave His message to the world; at Calvary He gave His life for the world. Human indebtedness increased daily; yet when the disciples had their greatest opportunity of expressing their gratitude, they miserably failed. There came a day when Christ urgently needed help; when a cruel cross had crushed Him to the ground. In those moments of supreme opportunity, the disciples refused to respond, and it was " a stranger coming out of the country " who carried the cross after Jesus.

The Shouldering of the Cross

Simon the Cyrenian lived in North Africa, but in common with all other people of his race he loved to attend the feasts at Jerusalem. This he was able to do because he had two sons who were capable of managing family affairs while he was away. Greatly excited, Simon completed the long journey and drew near to the city of his fathers. The temple roof glistening in the sunshine, the surging crowds, and the city itself, made sacred by the ministry of all the prophets, increased the thrill in his soul. He pressed along the street and came to the soldiers who at that moment were seeking the services of a strong man. " And as they came out, they found a man of Cyrene, Simon by name: him they *compelled* to bear his cross " (Matt. 27:32). There was no court of appeal against the injustice of the soldiers' request. These men were a law unto themselves, and even the other Jews laughed at the stranger's embarrassment. Simon was probably angry. It seemed inexcusable that they should inflict upon him the indignity of carrying a cross for a malefactor. His arguments were useless—" They compelled him to carry the cross." Perhaps God looked down and smiled. Such service would be amply rewarded. When the cross was lifted, the Saviour slowly arose and with quiet dignity gazed upon His helper. Sullenly, Simon returned the look, and in seeing the face of Jesus, he looked into the heart of God.

The Shame of the Cross

We can understand the reluctance of the Cyrenian; but another problem arises. Where were the disciples in this hour of crisis? They had promised to be true to their Master; they had vowed to go with Him both to prison and to death—where were they now? Probably they were standing in the crowd watching the unfolding of the sad drama, but when conscience suggested their going to aid the Lord, fear made them cowards. They were ashamed and afraid. To make a public confession of loyalty would invite the scorn of the entire multitude; they therefore left Him to suffer alone. Had any disciple rushed forward to lift the cross, he would have won eternal honours. Alas, they were all ashamed to respond, and the task was left to the man from Africa. He listened to the words addressed to the sorrowful women (Luke 23:28), and then followed to Calvary. He heard the request of the thief, and the response of Jesus; he listened as the Lord prayed, "Father, forgive them, for they know not what they do," and finally marvelled at the confession of the centurion who said, "Certainly this was the Son of God." And by this time his anger had died.

The Sight of the Cross

Was it true? Had he carried a cross for the Son of God? What did it all mean? And perhaps God smiled again. He knows how to reward His workmen, and is never in debt to any man. The work commenced at Calvary was completed in the garden tomb. The news of the resurrection brought new excitement to the city, and more particularly to Simon. Soon he heard another message: "If any man will come after me, let him deny himself, and take up his cross daily, and follow me." When Simon lifted the second cross, he was more than compensated for his task in carrying the first one. Alexander and Rufus are mentioned later in the New Testament, and all Bible teachers are in agreement that these leaders in the Church were the sons of the man who carried the cross for Christ. Who led them to the Saviour? Why, father, of course! God not only paid His debt, He gave "good measure, pressed down and running over." He always does.

THE THIEF . . . who found more than he ever stole
(LUKE 23:42, 43)

John Wesley once said, "Conversion is a work of God's grace in the heart," and nothing short of this can be conversion. It is a supernatural event resulting from a new vision. This is perfectly represented in the account of the thief's conversion. Against the sombre background of excruciating pain, this poor man had cursed the figure on the central cross. Then an indefinable charm emanated from the Lord. It seemed a balm from heaven, and before its soothing power, the fever cleared from the brain of the sinner.

He Saw Royalty in Jesus

"Lord," he cried, "remember me when thou comest into *thy kingdom,*" and at that precise moment no other person in the world believed in the kingship of Christ. Thirty-three years earlier the wise men had thrilled all Jewry with their announcement of the Messiah's birth. Much had happened since that memorable night. The wise men were no longer present. Later, the rugged disciples had gone forth boldly to proclaim the coming of the Kingdom; but Calvary had ruined their faith. Then, Pilate either in mockery or to annoy his Jewish opponents, had written a title: "This is Jesus of Nazareth, the King of the Jews," and had nailed it to the Cross. Yet, apparently he had no real faith whatsoever. No one believed Jesus to be the king—except the thief, and *he was sure.* How did he find out?

He Saw Resurrection in Jesus

"Lord, remember me when *thou comest into thy kingdom.*" Dead men do not have kingdoms, and it is well for us to remember that the thief saw a dying Jesus who seemed far more likely to inherit a tomb. "No," cried the sinner, "this is not the end of you. Somewhere, sometime, you will rise again and enter into your kingdom. When it happens, will you think of me?"

This is most remarkable, since no other was so rich in knowledge. The Lord Jesus had often foretold both His death and resurrection, but His words were remembered only by His enemies. "This deceiver said He would rise again," and to protect the body, they arranged for a guard to watch the tomb. Many of the people of the nation did not even think of an after-life, for the Sadducees believed death to be the termination of all existence. How then could anybody rise from the dead? The dying thief scorned such views. He knew Jesus would rise again to inherit a great kingdom. How could he be so sure?

He Saw Redemption in Jesus

"Lord, remember me—*me*. I am but a poor despicable sinner, and am unable to take any lamb to the priest. I cannot obey the commands of the law, but it matters not. O Lord, thou canst be to me both lamb and priest. Thou art able to get me into the kingdom. My sins will not be an insurmountable barrier if thou wilt be my offering; the law will never pass sentence on me if thou wilt be my advocate. O Lord, remember me."

What vision! We learned these things from the sacred Gospel record; but the thief had no Testament, and yet he knew. Whence came such knowledge? Surely God revealed it to him. His triple confession of guilt, need, and faith, had prepared the way for the Holy Spirit to illumine his soul. The sinner opened his heart, and the Saviour opened the door into the Kingdom. "To-day shalt thou be with Me in paradise." O grave, where is thy victory? O death, where is thy sting? Thanks be unto God, who giveth us the victory through our Lord Jesus Christ. That day the thief found more than he had ever stolen.

Happy man—and happy shall we be if we make a similar discovery.

> There is a fountain filled with blood,
> Drawn from Immanuel's veins;
> And sinners plunged beneath that flood
> Lose all their guilty stains.
>
> The dying thief rejoiced to see
> That fountain in his day;
> And there may I, though vile as he
> Wash all my sins away.

THE THIEF . . . who lost more than he ever regained

I fear that our interpretation of the conversion of the dying thief is a little one-sided. Far be it that we should ever under-estimate the marvel of forgiving grace; but the fact remains that some things are impossible even to the grace of God. We adore the Master, and gratefully remember how His wonderful words brought hope to the heart of this guilty man; but we must recognize that some sad features of the man's record remained unaltered. He had gained immeasurably—he had lost even more.

He had Lost his Life

We do not know the complete details of the man's life-story. His boyhood days had been spent in some home, and from that place of memory he had drifted on the currents of sin. Vice and folly had been characteristic of his actions, and in company with others of his type, he had gone from bad to worse. His evil life was destined to lead to his downfall. He was captured, brought to trial, and led to the place of execution. Then, when all seemed lost, the arms of God lifted him from the depths of depression, and the promise of Christ offered eternal assurance. Yet even God could not restore the years he had wasted. The man's life had vanished for ever. We have only one life to live, and when it is terminated we shall surely look in retrospect and mourn our failures. A life lost cannot be regained.

He had Lost his Opportunities

Perhaps it will not be inexcusable if we imagine for a moment what might have happened had the thief been granted a last-minute stay of execution. He might have become one of the greatest evangelists ever to tell the story of Jesus. Of course, this is mere speculation, but the sincerity of his pardoned soul would yearn for an opportunity of serving his Saviour. If only he could have returned to his former associates in crime, in order to preach the Gospel. Would his ministry have proved successful? Who can tell? The truth remains that with his life had gone all his opportunities—except one. He desperately seized what remained, and thus became the only man to speak in defence of the Saviour. He looked across at his brother thief and cried, " Dost not thou fear God, seeing thou art in the same condemnation? And we indeed justly, for we receive the due reward of our deeds: *but this man hath* done nothing amiss." Well done, thief, we are proud of you! " Ah," he whispers, " if only I had the chance to do more." But there were no further opportunities. Alas, he was too late, and went into eternity empty-handed—except for his Saviour's handclasp.

He had Lost his Eternal Rewards

We are not given many facts concerning the life here-after, but among those revealed is one great truth. We shall not all be on the same level of importance in heaven. Our works will be tried in the fires of divine scrutiny. " Every man's work shall be made manifest: for the day shall declare it, because it shall be revealed by fire, and the fire shall try every man's work of what sort it is. If a man's work abide . . . he shall receive a reward. If any man's work shall be burned, he shall suffer loss, but he himself shall be saved, yet so as by fire " (1 Cor. 3:13-15; Luke 14:14; Dan. 12:2, 3). My eternal destiny is settled by my faith. My eternal state is to be determined by the quality of service I may render in this life. The thief went home to heaven with nothing but his own faith. He had postponed his decision until time for service was non-existent. He gained much when Christ said, "To-day shalt thou be with me," but he had also lost far more than tongue can tell. And let this be a warning to us. Paul urged his fellow-Christians so to live that they would be unashamed at Christ's coming. *Now is the time to remember his words.*

> Must I go—and empty-handed?
> Must I meet my Saviour so?
> Not one soul with which to greet Him?
> Must I empty-handed go?
>
> Oh, ye saints, arouse, be earnest!
> Up and work while yet 'tis day;
> Ere the night of death o'ertake you,
> Strive for souls while yet you may.

CANA'S WEDDING . . . and the water that blushed

There are at least two reasons why this is one of the most interesting stories in the New Testament. (i) *Its details are interesting.* Here we have the account of two unknown people who requested the presence of Christ at their wedding. Their desire was so great that although Jesus was accompanied by His disciples, the young people gladly extended the additional invitations. The Lord Jesus left the more serious side of His great mission in order to join the happy throng in Cana of Galilee, where His presence added to the enjoyment of all the guests. During the festivities He performed His first miracle. It was destined to be the forerunner of many more. (ii) *Its interpretations are interesting.* John Wesley is reputed to have once said, " The water looked at Jesus and blushed." Modern commentators have said the water remained unaltered—that Jesus treated the entire episode as a joke, and supplied what is now termed " Adam's ale." To many other people who love their wine, this was the greatest of all Christ's miracles, and their only regret is their inability to emulate His example.

He Demonstrated His Power to Save

As far as we know this was the first crisis ever handled by Jesus, and it provided a great example of all that was to follow. This is a story of a crisis in family life, when the best-laid plans were beginning to miscarry; when an outstanding day was in danger of being ruined; when talkative people could so easily turn a molehill of disappointment into a mountain of trouble. The supply of wine had run short; the embarrassed host had underestimated his requirements, and was suddenly confronted with the problem of renewing supplies at short notice. When Jesus turned the water into wine, He not only performed His first miracle; He also rescued a family from extreme embarrassment. This was not the last occasion when His timely intervention helped to solve family problems. When the fellowship of Mary and Martha seemed at an end, His words restored new supplies of joy. If our domestic happiness or financial security should seem to be in jeopardy, we shall be wise in reporting our worries to Christ. If He cannot solve our problems, no one else can.

He Demonstrated His Power to Satisfy

"When the ruler of the feast had tasted the water that was made wine, and knew not whence it was . . . he called the bridegroom, and said . . . Thou hast kept the good wine until now." The change in quality could not pass unnoticed, for man cannot equal the Saviour's ability to produce vintage of real satisfaction. The Gospel story provided other examples of this type. When the Samaritan woman was about to offer a drink to Jesus, He responded with the startling information that He was able to supply a well of water within her soul. He said, "The water that I shall give shall be in you a well of living water, springing up into everlasting life." Some time later the disciples of John Baptist came to tell of the murder of their beloved leader. He spoke words of great comfort to them, and possibly the sorrowful men lingered in His presence and eventually became some of His additional disciples. And none would deny that the service of Jesus provided greater fellowship than anything hitherto known.

He Demonstrated His Power to Sustain

"Jesus saith unto them, Fill the waterpots with water. And they filled them up to the brim. And He saith unto them, *Draw out now,* and bear unto the governor of the feast. And they bare it." There has been difference of teaching in regard to the interpretation of the command "draw out now." Some people think the servants were commanded to draw from the waterpots; others think they were told to draw from the well. *Faith can take wine from a well even when all earlier attempts only obtained water.* Yet in any case Christ certainly provided sufficient supplies to meet the requirements of the emergency. His well of supply could never run dry while urgency of need moved the arm of faith. He was able to save, to satisfy, and to sustain His people. We are told that He is the same yesterday, and to-day, and for ever. There is therefore no need to emulate Hagar's example, to exist on the meagre allowance of a bottle filled with water. Let us ask God to reveal His well (Gen. 21 : 14-19)!

NICODEMUS ... who should have known better

No Bible picture appeals more to the imagination than that of the night visit made to Jesus by Nicodemus. He was *the* teacher of Israel, and we are justified in assuming he knew a great deal concerning Jewish theology, and might have helped in giving instruction to students. He was a famous minister, and John 7:50 reveals that he held a place entitling him to speak in the counsels of the nation. His knowledge of the writings of Daniel would enable him to understand that the coming of Messiah was overdue. The Anointed One should now be a grown man. This knowledge, and the presence of the amazing Carpenter, disturbed the thinker, and when opportunity occurred he went forth to seek the Lord.

How New

A few discreet inquiries; a gentle tap at a door; a whispered question; and eventually Nicodemus was shown into the presence of Jesus. The moment overwhelmed him. He offered no explanation of his late call; he asked no questions, and only succeeded in repeating that which his fellow-countrymen had been saying for months. " Rabbi, we know that thou art a teacher come from God: for no man can do these miracles that thou doest, except God be with him." Then suddenly his speech failed, and he did not even ask, " Are you more than a teacher sent from God? " Gravely the Master looked at him and said, " Except a man be born again, he cannot see the kingdom of God." This message was so foreign to the teachings of Israel, that even this learned Rabbi seemed at a loss. He thought Christ referred to physical rejuvenation. He should have known better, for the Jewish Scriptures were not silent concerning the theme. God greatly desired to give eternal life to man, and had symbolized this in the tree of life placed in the garden of Eden. When man partook of the forbidden fruit, sin entered his soul; had he partaken of the other tree, he would have received eternal life (Gen. 3:22). He lost that early opportunity because of his own sin; nevertheless the desires of God remained unchanged. Nicodemus should have known this from his study of the Scriptures.

How Necessary

Did the Saviour place a little emphasis on the second word of His sentence? Ye *must* be born again. The Jewish leader was greatly interested. As a man gives life to his child, and the child is born and thus begins to live, so the heavenly Father transmits eternal life to the soul; the soul is born again, and immediately enters into a new experience. This operation of divine grace is unquestionably essential, for " except a man be born again, he cannot see the kingdom of God." Observance of religious ritual, conformity to ancient or modern Church law, and even a high standard of morality, are insufficient. However much I succeed in beautifying my old nature, it still remains my old nature. Man's greatest need is not reformation, but regeneration. He needs a new life. Jesus affirmed that this was absolutely necessary, and any rejection of His teaching is fraught with the greatest danger. " Ye *must* be born again."

How Near

Did the face of the listening minister register surprise when he was politely but firmly reminded of his own need? *Ye* must be born again. The man whose weekly duties took him to the pulpit had need equally as great as that of the people to whom he preached. Wisely Nicodemus accepted the message and asked for further enlightenment. " How can such things be?" Great Teacher, if the heavenly Father desires to give eternal life, please tell me how this takes place. Christ's answer was sublime. " As Moses lifted up the serpent in the wilderness, even so must the Son of man be lifted up: that whosoever believeth in Him should not perish, but have everlasting life."

> There is life for a look at the crucified One,
> There is life at this moment for thee;
> Then look, sinner, look unto Him and be saved,
> Unto Him who was nailed to the tree.

THE WOMAN OF SAMARIA . . . who ran away with a well
(JOHN 4:14)

It was midday, and an atmosphere of lazy indolence filled the town as an outcast woman drew near to Sychar's well to draw water. She was accustomed to come at this hour, for the absence of scornful citizens made this the most appropriate time to obtain supplies from the well. As she drew near she saw the Stranger, and heard his request for water. "Then said the woman of Samaria unto Him, How is it that thou, being a Jew, asketh drink of me, which am a woman of Samaria? for the Jews have no dealings with the Samaritans. . . . And His disciples marvelled that He talked with the woman."

PROPOSITION 1. *The Love of God knows no racial barriers*

Between the woman and the Saviour were great barriers of social, racial, and spiritual differences. They were as unlike as it was possible to be, and it was not a cause for amazement that she expressed surprise at His actions. No other Jew would have acted similarly. Even the disciples had yet to learn that divisions were not permitted in the family of God. "There is neither Greek nor Jew, circumcision nor uncircumcision, Barbarian, Scythian, bond nor free: but Christ is all and in all" (Col. 3:11). The love of God sweeps away all barriers dividing His children, for baptized into the same family, we own God as our Father and each other as brethren. When the Lord Jesus looked into the eyes of a sinner, he saw a potential child of the Highest; it was therefore in keeping with the high ideals of His ministry that He should make special efforts to reach this outcast of society.

PROPOSITION 2. *The Provision of God knows no human limitations*

"The woman saith unto him, Sir, thou hast nothing to draw with, and the well is deep: from whence then hast thou that living water? . . . Jesus answered and said unto her, Whosoever drinketh of this water shall thirst again: But whosoever drinketh of the water that I shall give him shall never thirst; but the water that I shall give him shall be in him a well of water springing up into everlasting life." The words of Jesus were most strange to the listening woman. Without well, waterpots, or any other means of obtaining supplies, He calmly announced His ability to implant unending supplies within human breasts. The question regarding His superiority to Jacob surely produced an entrancing smile, for He knew Jacob would have valued the privilege of worshipping at His feet. Unaware of the identity of her companion, the woman said, "Sir, give me this water." Christ replied, "Go, call thy husband, and come hither."

PROPOSITION 3. *The Vision of God knows no undiscovered secrets*

"The woman answered and said, I have no husband. Jesus said unto her, Thou hast well said, I have no husband: for thou hast had five husbands, and he whom thou now hast is not thy husband: in that saidst thou truly. The woman saith unto Him, I perceive that thou art a prophet." Thus gradually her eyes began to open. She had requested living water, but this could not be granted until she had learned more of the Lord Jesus. Only faith can draw living water from the wells of God's salvation. With startling accuracy Christ's words revealed that her secrets were fully known to Him; yet He did not utter words of condemnation. His actions contrasted strangely with those of the self-righteous citizens whose attitude forced the woman to visit the well at midday. "She said, I know that Messias cometh, which is called Christ: when He is come, He will tell us all things."

PROPOSITION 4. *The Power of God knows no insurmountable obstacles*

"Jesus said unto her, I that speak unto thee am He." Momentarily surprised by the immensity of His claim, she eventually understood His words, and abandoning her waterpots, rushed into the city to spread the great news. A well of joy filled her soul as she exclaimed, "Come, see a man who told me all things that ever I did. Is not this the Christ?" Her testimony thrilled the citizens, and after two days of listening to Christ, they also shared her faith. The words of Christ had brought peace to their homes and radiance to their hearts.

THE NOBLEMAN . . . who did not go home

(JOHN 4:52)

This is one of the most charming illustrations of the way in which a man may seek and find the Saviour. The various milestones along the path of experience are clearly seen, and tell of a nobleman whose faith attained to true greatness. Let us accompany him through the changing emotions of his supreme achievement.

He Needed Christ

The house was a place of increasing anxiety, for even the servants knew that the child was at the point of death. Undoubtedly the best medical advice had been obtained, yet it seemed impossible to prevent the death of the little boy. We must try to understand how the distressed father grieved when he looked into the pale, strained face of his darling son. Then someone mentioned that Jesus had come again to Cana in Galilee, a town approximately twenty miles away. Furthermore, it was rumoured that additional miracles of healing had taken place. The anxious man looked again at his child, and realized how great was his need of Jesus. Possibly pride struggled momentarily against the humility of bowing before a Nazarene carpenter, but love triumphed as the nobleman hurried along the dusty road.

He Sought Christ

Somewhere in distant Cana the Master waited, and eventually the nobleman walked into His presence. Every bystander wondered what reason could account for his coming. "He besought Jesus that He would come down and heal his son: for he was at the point of death. Then said Jesus unto him, Except ye see signs and wonders, ye will not believe. The nobleman saith unto Him, Sir, come down ere my child die." And so the man prayed. Anything can happen when a sincerely desperate soul bows at the feet of the Saviour.

> Did ever saint find this Friend forsake him?
> Or sinner find that He would not take him?
> No, not one!

The great man was very wise in carrying his need to Christ.

He Believed Christ

" Jesus said unto him, Go thy way; thy son liveth. And the man believed the word that Jesus had spoken unto him, and went his way." *But obviously he did not go home.* According to Jewish time, the miracle took place at one o'clock in the afternoon—the seventh hour. Some people have suggested that Roman time was being used —seven o'clock in the morning. It really does not matter which is correct, for it is evident that the man did not return to his home until the following day. He could have been home either by six o'clock in the evening, in the one instance, or otherwise, in time for lunch. But he did neither! Why did he not return immediately? Surely he wanted to see his boy. The nobleman either stayed to listen to the great Teacher, or went to a nearby inn to sleep—probably he had not slept for nights. And if anyone had asked why he did not go home, he would have answered: " There is no need to hurry home. The Master said my little boy is well, and I believe what Jesus says." At home the servants continued to wait, but when the father failed to appear they set out to look for him. When they met he asked when the child had recovered, and they said, " *Yesterday* at the seventh hour the fever left him." Such was the reward of true faith.

He Confessed Christ

I should have loved to be present at the homecoming. I almost see the little boy running to jump into his daddy's arms; and I am wondering if emotion robbed the father of immediate speech. Then the servants, and possibly other members of the family, came in to hear the story. Every detail of the account increased their amazement. And as the sense of the presence of God became increasingly evident, hearts were humbled and heads were bowed: " And the nobleman believed, and his whole house." Such grand tidings could never be confined within the limits of one human heart. This wonderful Jesus had saved them. Why should they be ashamed to sound forth His praises? Let all Capernaum know; let all Judea know; let the whole world know. " Sir, across the centuries we stretch forth the hand of friendship. We hail you not merely as a nobleman, but as a noble man unashamed of our blessed Saviour."

THE ADULTERESS . . . and the writings of Christ

(JOHN 8:6)

This Bible story suggests a most interesting question. What message did Jesus write? It is the only recorded instance of its type, and people of many lands have speculated as to the nature of His words. It appears that a foul plot had been planned to incriminate Jesus. Possibly a crafty lawyer had schemed a way—a seemingly infallible way—of trapping the Saviour. A sinful woman who had been taken in adultery was publicly accused before Christ.

SUGGESTION 1

" And when they had set her in the midst, they say unto Him, Master, this woman was taken in adultery, in the very act. Now Moses in the law commanded us, that such should be stoned: but what sayest thou?" We must realize the subtlety of this evil scheme. If Jesus had answered, " All right, stone her," the common people would probably have accused Him of preaching what He did not practise. He taught that God loved sinners. On the other hand, if He forbade the stoning, His enemies could order His arrest for contempt of the law. The Lord was never hurried. He calmly stooped down and wrote on the ground. Did He write the true saying of Moses? (Lev. 20:10). The great lawgiver had declared that if people were taken in adultery, *both* guilty parties should be stoned to death. The accusation stated that the woman had been taken *in the act*. Why, then, had the captors allowed the man to escape? Obviously this was a premeditated plan—not to clean a city, but to trap Jesus.

SUGGESTION 2

It might have been that Jesus wrote some of the secrets of their own past life. If this be the case, how easy it is to understand why, when He said, " He that is without sin among you, let him first cast a stone at her," they went out one by one, beginning at the eldest, even to the last. The eldest probably had most to hide. If Jesus had indicated that He was aware of their secret sins, they would be afraid to commence the stoning lest He denounce them as hypocrites. They were unprepared to face such a denunciation, and seized the opportunity to slip away.

SUGGESTION 3

Perhaps He wrote some of the great passages from their own Scriptures stating that God was full of compassion and overflowing in mercy. He may have reminded them of David, and other important leaders whose sins were magnified by the greatness of their office. Yet God had mercy on the guilty. If He could be gracious, His people should follow the example. Perhaps Christ wrote all three of these suggestions; and while He wrote, slowly a sinful woman awakened to the realization that He was completely different from any she had ever known. Her life-story might be written under six headings: Her fall, fear, Friend, faith, forgiveness, and future. And in the outworking of these we find another problem. Why did Christ say to her, "Neither do I condemn thee"? Holiness had no alternative but to condemn the woman. Unless we can find some reason for this gracious act of Jesus, other Scriptures will seem meaningless.

SUGGESTION 4

"When Jesus had lifted up Himself, and saw none but the woman, He said unto her, Woman, where are those thine accusers? hath no man condemned thee? She said, No man, Lord."—Lord—LORD. We are told that no man can call Him "Lord" but by the Holy Spirit. Slowly the work of enlightenment had been progressing in her soul, and finally she realized He was not an ordinary man—He was the Lord. Faith had been born within her heart, and such faith can remove mountains—even mountains of sin. It was only then that Christ said, "Neither do I condemn thee: go and sin no more." "There is therefore now no condemnation to them which are in Christ Jesus." When God forgives, He forgets; and the feet of this woman had already reached the path of grace. She had commenced her new life.

> Grace is flowing like a river,
>   Millions there have been supplied;
> Still it flows as fresh as ever
>   From the Saviour's wounded side.

THE BLIND MAN . . . whose hand I must shake in heaven

(JOHN 9:35-38)

In the ninth chapter of John's gospel we have the remarkable record of the growth of a soul. It provides a most fascinating study. A blind beggar who daily sat in the gateway of his city, suddenly felt clay placed upon his eyes and heard the strange command, " Go, wash in the pool of Siloam. He went his way therefore, and came seeing." Soon afterwards he became the centre of a great crowd of people arguing about his identity. The Pharisees argued about the breaking of the Sabbath; the crowd about the man. Then someone approached the beggar and asked how such healing had taken place. The reply enables us to understand the beggar's first conception of the Saviour.

A Man that is Called Jesus (v. 11)

Let us try to understand things from the beggar's point of view. He was not a theological student, and seems to have been just a poor man. A voice of indescribable sweetness had suggested the journey to the pool, and in responding he had received his sight. At first his entire conception of the Stranger was that he had been a man who had paused on the roadside to speak to him. This, of course, was perfectly correct, but no sincere convert can ever stay at such a low level of comprehension. If Christ be only a man, we are obliged to admit He was a very strange man. He claimed to be the Messiah, and the Scriptures had already declared of the coming Messiah: " His name shall be called . . . The mighty God, The everlasting Father . . ." (Isa. 9:6). When a mere man claims to be equal with God, he betrays signs of insanity.

He is a Prophet (v. 17)

The heated arguments continued, until the crowd divided. Feelings were somewhat strained when certain of the people again asked the blind man, " What sayest thou of Him, that He hath opened thine eyes? He said, He is a prophet." A little reflection had enabled the beggar to realize that his benefactor was more than an ordinary man. He ranked with the great men of Jewish history. He was a prophet, who spoke with the authority of the Most High. The crowd then visited the home of the beggar, and soon a new storm of angry discussion burst over his head. He had had no time to enjoy his new experience, for immediately he had become the storm centre of animated debate.

He is my Master (v. 27)

"Then said they to him again, What did He to thee? how opened He thine eyes? He answered them, I have told you already, and ye did not hear: wherefore would ye hear it again? will ye *also* be His disciples?" We must consider the word *also*. It represented a man's confession that he had decided to follow Jesus. If the ancient prophets had disciples, this prophet would also have them; and as far as the beggar was concerned, he intended to be one of them. The Jews were quick to understand the meaning of his words, for they replied, "Thou art his disciple; but we are Moses' disciples." Then the convert commenced preaching, and his powers of reasoning so confounded his critics they could only say in reply, "Thou wast altogether born in sins, and dost thou teach us? And they cast him out."

Jesus the Son of God (v. 38)

"Jesus heard that they had cast him out; *and when He had found him,* He said unto him, Dost thou believe on the Son of God?" The Lord Jesus was most gracious in seeking the poor outcast; but let us remember that the beggar had never seen the face of Christ, and could hardly be expected to recognize the Stranger. He probably wrestled with his thoughts before he replied, "Who is He, Lord, that I might believe on Him? And Jesus said . . . It is He that talketh with thee. And he said, Lord, I believe. And he worshipped Him." I shall want to discuss many problems with this man when some day I shall meet him in heaven. I shall ask if he became one of the additional disciples when the original twelve were increased to seventy. Yes, I think I shall enjoy meeting this fine fellow; and if earth's customs have not been forgotten, I shall grip his hand hard, for I'm thrilled at his refusal to be brow-beaten by those bombastic leaders. Well done, brother! I wish I'd been there.

MARY OF BETHANY . . . and the eclipse in her soul

This is one of the most human stories of the Bible, and its counterparts may be found in every city of the world. Tragedy has lain bare the noble soul of Mary of Bethany, for two crushing blows have fallen upon her. Her brother has died; and *Jesus of Nazareth has failed her.* " Now a certain man named Lazarus was sick. . . . Therefore his sisters sent unto Jesus, saying, Lord, behold he whom thou lovest is sick." And with that statement went the hopes and prayers of two sincere hearts.

The Strange Delay

" When Jesus had heard therefore that Lazarus was sick, He abode two days still in the same place where He was." The messenger was permitted to return alone, and the apparent indifference of the Saviour surely dealt a most painful blow to those who anxiously awaited His coming. When Lazarus died, the grief of his sisters was greatly intensified—Jesus had failed them. To them, His action seemed both heartless and inexcusable. Each time Mary considered the problem, the tendency to grow bitter increased in her soul. Perhaps only the people who have similarly suffered will appreciate her anguish. The problems of sickness and suffering are ever before us; but when eager, anxious prayers remain unanswered, even the strongest faith can be shaken. The Lord Jesus deliberately stayed away, and in her acute disappointment Mary forgot to consider that His action might have been dictated by wisdom.

The Suggestive Delay

" Then after that saith He to His disciples, Let us go into Judæa again. . . . Then Martha, as soon as she heard that Jesus was coming, went and met Him: *but Mary sat still in the house.*" Why did she linger at home? Her sister went to meet the Lord, and the entire world knows of the confession that soon fell from her lips. But when Jesus asked about Mary, Martha had to explain the cause of her sister's absence. And is it not most significant how

Jesus abruptly discontinued his walk toward the beloved home? When Mary eventually came to Him, "Jesus was not yet come into the town, *but was in that place where Martha met him*" (v. 30). He commissioned Martha to carry His message: "The Master is come, and calleth for thee." Why did He not accompany Martha, and so save time? The Lord Jesus was very wise. The raising of Lazarus would not be as difficult as the healing of a wounded soul. Was Mary a little bitter? Was she still hurt because Christ had failed to respond in the hour of her greatest need? The new delay, the delay in Christ's entry into the town, is most suggestive. When Mary heard that Jesus was calling for her, her great love swept aside all hindrances and she arose and came quickly.

The Sublime Delay

And when Jesus came to the tomb, "He lifted up his eyes, and said, Father, I thank thee that thou hast heard me." The prayer of the Saviour was all-embracing. The vision of man might have been limited to the tomb, and the possibility of a miracle; He looked beyond, to the transformation taking place in the hearts of His followers. Until that day He had been to the Bethany family a friend, and a possible Messiah; but Martha had now exclaimed, "Yea, Lord, I believe that thou art the Christ, the Son of God, which should come into the world." Some day, Lazarus will die again; but if Jesus be the Son of God, new meaning would be found in His message, "Let not your heart be troubled . . . I go to prepare a place for you . . . that where I am there ye may be also." The victory won in their souls that day far exceeded the triumph obtained at the tomb. It was for this reason that Christ delayed His response to the sisters' prayer. Had He immediately responded, they would have lost their greatest blessing. The eclipse was but a shadow, it passed away, and Mary's path to the sunshine was clearly revealed. *She heard* (v. 29); *she came* (v. 32); *she saw* (v. 32); *she fell at His feet* (v. 32).

Her pathway has never become overgrown. It remains open for all weary travellers.

THE THREE MARYS . . . who lingered at the Cross
(JOHN 19:25)

" Now there stood by the cross of Jesus His mother, and His mother's sister, Mary the wife of Cleophas, and Mary Magdalene." If I were a woman this would be one of my favourite texts. When most of the disciples had forsaken Christ, three women lingered in His presence. They were all named Mary. If we could link this verse with 1 Corinthians 13:13, where the triple attributes of faith, hope, and love are mentioned, then we might be able to present each of the three women with a surname, for a little investigation reveals that they travelled to the cross along different pathways.

MARY FAITH—His mother

The story of Joseph's wife is among the loveliest stories in the world. Faced with the physical impossibility of Christ's conception, she believed and said, " Be it unto me according to thy word," and in joyful anticipation sang, " My soul doth magnify the Lord." His subsequent coming, and the cumulative testimony of the shepherds, the wise men, the prophet Simeon, and the prophetess Anna, only increased the wonderment of her heart. Later, she heard the boy Jesus name God as His Father; and by the time He was thirty she had sufficiently grown in faith to be able confidently to expect His first miracle (John 2:5). She had no doubt, for she had come to realize the extent of His power. Alas, her faith was soon to suffer. The Pharisees came asking about His age and accusing Him of blasphemy. Mary gathered together her other children, and went seeking Him. It is said that His kinsmen thought He was beside Himself, and would have taken Him home (Mark 3:21, 31). Then came the cross, and any remaining thought of His divinity disappeared. Mary went away, and as far as we know never returned until the news of the resurrection electrified everybody.

MARY HOPE—the wife of Cleophas

The entire background of this woman's experience is different. She was the wife of a disciple who is also mentioned in the account of the walk to Emmaus. Possibly in common with many other people, she had rallied to His cause firmly believing Him to be the promised Messiah. Each miracle added fuel to the fires of her hopes; but as with the first Mary, the tragedy of the cross devastated her soul. It is more than likely that she was the unknown companion accompanying Cleophas back to the home in Emmaus, and their testimony to the Stranger is most illuminating. They said, "We trusted it had been he which should have redeemed Israel." Such hopes would have perished but for the resurrection.

MARY LOVE—Magdalene

If Magdalene is to have a surname, it must be Love. She had known the misery of being possessed by devils, and then Jesus had brought heaven to her soul. The memory of His unsurpassed kindness and power thrilled her, as every day with other women she followed ministering to Him. She also had faith, and fervently hoped He would be the Messiah; yet underneath lay something greater. She loved Him. Had He failed? Had He been a blasphemer? People said so; but their opinions made no difference. She had loved Him in life; she loved Him in death, and perhaps that is the reason why she was the only one of the three Marys to come back on the morning of the resurrection. Primarily she did not return to worship a risen Lord; she came because she still loved the dead Jesus. "And now abideth faith, hope, love, these three: but the greatest of these is love." There is a faith— a mental assent that cannot survive a Calvary. There is a hope—that can be submerged by disappointment. But love is unchanging; it is eternal; it is like God. Such love brought the Saviour down to us; such love alone can take us up to Him.

Let me love Thee, Saviour,
Take my heart for ever:
Nothing but Thy favour
My soul can satisfy.

THE SOLDIERS . . . who portrayed a world

Somewhere near the city of Jerusalem was a military camp, the most dangerous garrison in the entire Roman empire. Its soldiers were not unaware of the greatness of their peril, for they had already tasted of the bitterness of the people whose land they occupied. Each night they talked around their camp fires, and the advent of Jesus into the life of the nation provided the most disturbing of all their themes. It was said He could even walk on the sea; that He could raise the dead. If such a man were to lead Israel, there would be serious trouble. As the feast time approached, every soldier looked to his weapons. Then came the most startling news of all. The enemy had rejected their king, and now desired his elimination. On the most fateful day in history, the soldiers went out to superintend the death of Jesus; and in the shadow of the cross their own individuality was soon displayed.

The Indifferent Man

" Then the soldiers, when they had crucified Jesus . . . took his coat . . . and said, Let us not rend it, but cast lots for it, whose it shall be " (John 19:23, 24). Some unknown character, possibly a woman, had woven a coat without a seam, and had presented it to her Lord. The soldiers coveted this treasure, and turning their backs on the cross cast lots for it. They were so interested in material things that they had little thought for Christ. Thus they foreran the materialist of the present day. There are folk who live for the sole purpose of increasing their wealth, and alas, are so poor they have nothing but money. Surely the only true test of wealth is to take away all material possessions, and then see what a man has left. True riches consist in abiding peace, rest of heart, and in the abundance of friends who remain true even in the hour of adversity. The soldiers were so short-sighted that they were unable to see beyond this opportunity of getting something for nothing.

The Incensed Man

" But when they came to Jesus, and saw that he was dead already, they brake not his legs; but one of the soldiers with a spear pierced his side " (John 19:33, 34). This represents one of the most callous acts of humanity, and we can only speculate as to the cause of the man's bitterness. The would-be persecutor actually thrust his spear into a dead body. It seems that he wanted to hurt Jesus, and was disgruntled because he had arrived too late to do as he had planned. Why was he so bitter? Perhaps he had had dealings with unscrupulous Jews, and in arrogant self-righteousness had classed all of that race in the same category. To him Jesus was just another Jew—someone to be hated. And are there not such people still living? Are there not multitudes who, having met a few hypocrites, vehemently scorn the Gospel and reject the Saviour? In many cases man's sense of justice has been warped by the prejudice and bitterness of his heart.

The Inspired Man

" And the centurion which stood over against Him . . . said, Truly this was the Son of God " (Mark 15:39). " Ah, wise man; the more I look at you, the more I like you. You heard the Lord asking His Father to forgive sinners; you listened to the request of the dying thief, and probably marvelled at the amazing response made by Jesus. I have always wondered if you were the same officer who earlier insisted that there was no necessity for Christ to enter a simple abode. He had only to speak the word, and the miracle would be accomplished. Some day in heaven I think I shall want to ask you that question. You were right, you know; He was the Son of God."

It is night time, and the three men are back in camp. The first proudly displays his winnings—a coat. The second bitterly nurses his grievance. The third, with a strange peace filling his heart, remembers the words of the Crucified. I see them so clearly now; but I wonder which I resemble most?

MAGDALENE . . . who walked toward the sunrise

Someone has said, "Little is much when God is in it," and every mention of Easter reminds one of the old proverb. There are several significant details about this thrilling resurrection story, but the most intriguing of all is the time factor of Magdalene's visit to the sepulchre. If we could sit in conference with the three authors, Matthew, Mark and John, we should be greatly interested to listen as they thrashed out their problem. They apparently disagreed about the time of Mary's memorable visit to the tomb.

Let John Tell Us

"Yes, brother, we would like to hear your version." The apostle smiles and points to his message in chapter 20:1. "The first day of the week cometh Mary Magdalene early, *when it was yet dark,* unto the sepulchre, and seeth the stone taken away from the sepulchre." With his quiet, clear voice of authority he declares, "She came when it was still dark," and his fathomless eyes seem to suggest this was true in a dual sense. The darkness of the city compared with the darkness of her soul. Her Friend and Master had been crucified, and by one cruel stroke of misfortune all her hopes had perished. Life could never be the same now that Christ was dead. She had awaited the passing of the sabbath, but so great was her desire to be near His tomb, she came when it was still dark.

Let Matthew Tell Us

We imagine Matthew's discreet little cough as he rises to tell his story. "My brother John, you are right and yet you are wrong. It was dark both within and without her soul, but another detail must be added to the story. Listen" . . . and Matthew carefully points to his own record (28:1). "'In the end of the sabbath, *as it began to dawn* toward the first day of the week, came Mary Magdalene . . . to see the sepulchre.' My brother John, it is true to say that she came when it was dark—*it was dark;* but as she continued toward the tomb, the shadows of the night commenced to flee. Signs of the approaching day were beginning to became visible. You will agree that this also became true of her deepest feelings. She did not know about the Lord's resurrection. He was dead, and with Him her joys had also been buried. Yet some urge took her to the tomb, and this proved one of the greatest events in her life. Yes, it is true for us all—the darkness disappears when we draw near to Him."

Let Mark Tell Us

Mark is smiling; he is the youngest of the three. He has often talked with Simon Peter, and seems sure of his facts. "Brethren, listen and I will read from my writings at 16:2. 'And very early in the morning the first day of the week, they came unto the sepulchre *at the rising of the sun.*' I am sorry, gentlemen, if I seem to disagree with you. No, do not misunderstand me; I am not suggesting that you are wrong. Perhaps it was dark when our sister commenced her journey; and brother Matthew, maybe it did begin to dawn as she drew nearer the tomb; but I am quite certain that the sun was rising as she came to the sepulchre. My brethren, a new day had begun." We seem to hear his deep chuckle as he continued, "Of course, a new day had begun. The Sun of Righteousness had arisen with healing in His wings; and may everlasting glory be to His holy name."

Let Us Tell Them

Are they startled to see people of a later age intruding upon the privacy of their conversation? Let us take courage. Are they not our older brethren? "Matthew and Mark and John, we are pleased to meet you. Your writings have often inspired us. We have been greatly interested in your animated conversation; but we desire to repeat one of our proverbs—'Little is much when God is in it.' The little differences in the time factor of your story thrilled us. Don't you realize that it took the three of you to write our story? We also knew what it meant to pass along the road leading from the darkness into the light of a new day. We also found a risen Lord, and have never ceased praising Him."

Dr. GAMALIEL . . . who foreran Mr. Asquith

(ACTS 5:38, 39)

Dear Dr. Gamaliel, we have always been profoundly interested in you. True greatness will always command respect, and the people of our generation readily admit you were one of the greatest figures of your time. The New Testament has faithfully recorded three vital things concerning you, and these have placed you high in our estimation. First, *you were had in respect of all the people.* Probably as head of the theological college you controlled the streams of culture which constantly flowed from your institution to all parts of the land. Secondly, *you were able to command in the great Jewish council.* We have wondered if you were the President, for few men could have such authority in such high circles. Thirdly, *your speech probably saved the lives of our early Christian brethren.* Even though your colleagues were intensely bitter, you miraculously poured oil on the troubled waters of that momentous meeting. We are all agreed, doctor, you were a great man.

Gamaliel the Doubtful

But we are puzzled about one or two things. Your high office suggests that you were not a newcomer to the public life of Israel. You were the head of the college, and one of the leaders of the Sanhedrin. You must have been present when the Lord Jesus appeared before the elders. Your eyes probably beheld all the sad events of those dread days, yet nowhere is it recorded that you said a word in defence of the nation's greatest benefactor. Your earlier silence contrasts with the excellent speech of later days, and we are driven to the conclusion that something had upset your former attitude. Whereas you were content to allow Jesus to die, you later admitted the possibility that His cause might have been of God. Dr. Gamaliel, what caused the change of outlook? Was it brought about by the resurrection and the resultant deeds of the transformed disciples? If so, we sympathize with you. The resurrection of Jesus was sufficient to disturb anyone.

Gamaliel the Careful

You remind us of a famous politician who, when confronted by a difficult problem, said, "We'll wait and see." His message has now entered into everyday speech. Yes, you and he might have been brothers. You said to your angry colleagues, "Refrain from these men and let them alone: for if this counsel or work be of men, it will come to nought: But if it be of God ye cannot overthrow it, lest haply ye be found even to fight against God." It was obvious even to the councillors that you preferred to wait and see. Yes, your advice was very sound. Sometimes fools rush in where angels fear to tread, and it would have been tragic indeed if such an august body of men had been committed to a policy soon to be revealed as stupid.

Gamaliel the Fearful

But just a moment. How long was your policy to remain in force? Did you advise waiting until sufficient evidence had been obtained enabling you to decide one way or the other? Ah, do you remember Saul of Tarsus? He was your student. At the conclusion of his training he went out to serve the cause of Judaism, and his deeds won the praise of all who countenanced brutality. Were you pleased when you heard of his murderous acts? And then something happened to him. Oh yes, you know what we mean. The persecutor became a preacher, and under his wonderful ministry the cause of Christ spread from shore to shore. It proved to be as you forecast—if it were of God no one could overthrow it. The cause of Judaism began to die, but the power of the Gospel swayed the world. Were you looking for evidence, Dr. Gamaliel? It seems shameful that your name does not appear in the lists of famous Christians. Did you shrink from the path of duty because of the fear of losing your position, your fame, your income, and possibly your life? Did you finish your days as a secret disciple, believing in your heart but ashamed to confess with your lips? Poor Dr. Gamaliel, we are so sorry for you. In such a fine fellow this flaw would cause endless unhappiness.

STEPHEN . . . the odd job man

(ACTS 6:2-5)

There was trouble in the Church, and unless preventative measures could be made quickly, it showed signs of developing into a first-class row. " And in those days, when the number of the disciples was multiplied, there arose a murmuring of the Grecians against the Hebrews, because their widows were neglected in the daily ministration. Then the twelve called the multitude of the disciples unto them, and said, It is not reason that we should leave the word of God, and serve tables. Wherefore, brethren, look ye out among you seven men of honest report, full of the Holy Ghost and wisdom, whom we may appoint over this business." We commend the action of the apostles, for their preparation of sermons left little time to devote to the menial tasks of dispensing physical necessities. They were not willing to leave the important work of preaching, and therefore urged that other suitable men be appointed to superintend the humbler activities of the Church. The multitude chose Stephen, and the choice was admirable—except for the fact that he was a more capable preacher than most of the apostles.

TESTIMONY 1. . . . *His Great Humility*

" Brother Stephen, there is discord in the assembly, and we are so busy preparing to preach, we would like you to lead a small committee responsible for the benevolent side of the Church. You are not a preacher, and therefore will have plenty of time in which to do this task. Do you mind? Of course not, you are an accommodating fellow. Now we shall have peace in which to study the word of God." Stephen smiled and approached his new task with the realization that he was to do this for his Lord. Many of his fellow-Christians would have been less willing had they possessed Stephen's gifts. He was a most excellent preacher, whose sermons and ability were almost unsurpassed. His conceptions of thought and argument were so outstanding that God faithfully recorded one of his sermons and gave it a place of honour—fifty-three verses of the seventh chapter of the Acts of the Apostles. He was a wonderful exponent of the Scriptures; yet he graciously concurred with the apostles' request to devote his time to serve at tables.

TESTIMONY 2. . . . *His Great Ministry*

" And Stephen, full of faith and power, did great wonders and miracles among the people " (Acts 6:8). Brother Stephen, we have been wondering how long it took the people to discover your true greatness. The common folk obviously had keen eyesight, and were delighted with your ministry of healing. Did the apostles say anything about the revival at the tables of the Church? Surely they were a little surprised when the Lord took you from the pantry to the pulpit. Your talents, dear brother, could not be wasted on the settlement of disputes when they were so urgently needed in the highest court of the nation. But we would like to ask a question—How did you manage to include so much Scripture in one sermon, and condense four thousand years of history into one short oration? You were not only filled with the Holy Spirit; you were also filled with the word of truth. It seems strange that you should ever have been the odd job man of the Church.

TESTIMONY 3. . . . *His Great Christlikeness*

You were the first to follow in the footsteps of the Lord, and your brothers and sisters in Christ have become very proud of you. We have read the immortal account of your homegoing—" When the Jews heard these things, they were cut to the heart, and they gnashed on him with their teeth. But he, being full of the Holy Ghost, looked up stedfastly into heaven, and saw the glory of God, and Jesus standing on the right hand of God . . . and they stoned Stephen, calling upon God, and saying, Lord Jesus, receive my spirit. And he kneeled down, and cried with a loud voice, Lord, lay not this sin to their charge. And when he had said this, he fell asleep." (i) Brother, you had excellent vision, for you saw the Saviour waiting to welcome you home. (ii) You had excellent grace—enough to forgive your enemies. (iii) You had excellent confidence —to place yourself in omnipotent hands, and then to fall asleep. Your promotion from the ranks was most rapid, for the Lord was quick to recognize greatness—even in a kitchen.

SIMON ... the church member who had never met Christ

(Acts 8:21)

Few men will ever experience the popularity enjoyed by Simon the sorcerer of Samaria. His fame had spread abroad and was known by all the people. Luke said of the man, " He bewitched the people of Samaria, giving out that himself was some great one: To whom they all gave heed, from the least to the greatest, saying, This man is the great power of God " (Acts 8:9, 10). We do not know how he practised his art, and thus cannot judge whether he was an expert magician or a genuine spiritist medium. He was known and respected by all men, and was one of the leading people of the city.

Simon the Convert

Samaria was one of the first places where Christian enterprise overcame the hardships of persecution. When the Church was driven from Jerusalem, the saints hastened to other places and began witnessing for their Lord. They did this in Samaria, and great blessing immediately fell upon the new work. Led by the untiring Philip, the new evangelists preached the Gospel, and revival reached the city. The people who had been enslaved to the wiles and sorceries of the great Simon, suddenly lost their fear, and hurried to the meetings to hear of the risen Christ. The horrors of persecution were forgotten as men sought for Christ. Daily the new Church increased in size, and there was much rejoicing when the old sorcerer apparently saw his need of Christ, responded to the message, and publicly confessed his faith in baptism. Immediately he regained all the popularity he had enjoyed hitherto. To the Samaritans it was a matter calling for praise that their leading citizen had unashamedly joined their ranks. His coming gave added impetus to the movement, and within a short time the story of the revival in Samaria had reached the apostles who had tarried in Jerusalem.

Simon the Covetous

" Now when the apostles which were at Jerusalem heard that Samaria had received the word of God, they sent unto them Peter and John: Who, when they had come down, prayed for them, that they might receive the Holy Ghost." The Christians were thrilled when they heard that two of the leading apostles were to continue the great work. The meetings were packed with eager, excited listeners, and all marvelled when the new preachers demonstrated the great power brought into their lives by the Holy Spirit. Simon the sorcerer was amazed when, through the laying on of the apostles' hands, the Holy Spirit was given to earnest seekers. But while other people in the congregation rejoiced and praised the Lord, the eyes of the old sorcerer looked hungrily toward the apostle Peter. Finally, he walked to the front and said, " Give me also this power, that on whomsoever I lay hands, he may receive the Holy Ghost." His eyes lit up with pride as he explained he was able to pay handsomely for the favour.

Simon the Condemned

" But Peter said unto him, Thy money perish with thee . . . Thou hast neither part nor lot in this matter: for *thy heart is not right in the sight of God*. Repent therefore of this thy wickedness . . for I perceive that thou art . . . *in the bond of iniquity*." If any of the young Samaritan converts overheard Peter's rebuke, their courage might have failed, for such drastic treatment could easily result in the loss of a most valuable Church member. The apostle grimly uttered his words. The man was still in his sin—the bond of iniquity. And since a Christian is never said to be " *in sin* " but rather " *in Christ*," here is the evidence that the sorcerer had never been saved. The man who had basked in the sunshine of men's favour had suddenly realized that the Church had taken away his followers. He therefore made profession of faith in Christ, and by so doing regained all he had lost. Yet although he joined the Church and was baptized before the people, neither his action nor the Church ordinance had removed the stain from his soul. He was still a lost sinner, and Peter did not hesitate to say so. The sorcerer did not argue with Peter, but fearfully asked that prayer might be made on his behalf. Poor man! His Church membership without a personal knowledge of Christ was as empty and as disappointing as a body without life.

SAUL ... the persecutor who became a preacher

The conversion of Saul of Tarsus was the greatest event in the history of the early Church. The fury of this man's attack upon the disciples had caused much pain and sorrow, and had plunged many homes into mourning. He seemed fanatically opposed to everything connected with the Saviour, and had become a terror to every believer. The news that such a fiend had surrendered to the Lord Jesus was unbelievable, and the saints were reluctant to approach the new convert. Transformed by the power of redeeming love, the persecutor lay in the dust of the Damascus highway, and his fellow-travellers quickly realized that his eyesight had been taken away. They led him into the city and brought him to the house of Judas. Eventually his eyes were opened, and with the new vision came certain clear realizations.

He Saw the Emptiness of a Christless Life

Even while he had remained blind his past had appeared before him, and in the time that elapsed before the arrival of Ananias, the troubled man had many opportunities for reflection. He had endeavoured to possess a conscience void of offence; he had faithfully observed the principles taught in the synagogue, and according to the law was blameless. Yet in spite of all his efforts to gain the approbation of God, frustration had thwarted his every effort, and his heart remained troubled and restless. Increasing religious fervour had not supplied peace to his soul, and at last he had begun to realize that not even religion could take the place of God's Son. Life—even the best life, without a personal acquaintance with Christ, was empty and purposeless.

He Saw the Necessity for Confessing his new Faith Openly

" And he received sight forthwith, and arose, and was baptized." New Testament baptism was a public act, and could be witnessed by all people. Saul resisted any thought of becoming a secret disciple, and openly proclaimed his acceptance of the new faith. He fully realized that all fellow-members of his nation recognized in baptism the sign that a decision had become final. Had he quietly remained a devoted convert and failed to observe the command of Christ to be baptized, his old associates would have endeavoured to persuade him to return to the faith of his fathers. His act of public baptism proclaimed to all that he had chosen to follow the Saviour, and no amount of persuasion would ever convince him of the necessity to abandon his new Master. He had unashamedly persecuted the Lord Jesus, and the only way to atone for his former atrocities was publicly to renounce his old life.

He Saw the Desirability of Christian Fellowship

" Then was Saul certain days with the disciples which were at Damascus." He could never forget how Ananias had entered into his room, saying, " Brother Saul." That his old enemies now recognized him as their brother seemed an amazing thing, and the more he lingered in the company of his new friends the more he liked them. They talked of the Lord Jesus, and through the medium of their ministry he grew in grace daily. Early in his career Paul thus learned the value of a Christian assembly, and ever afterwards he found delight in forming similar Churches. He always urged converts to be true to their Church, and " not to forsake the assembling of yourselves together." The world would be a poor place without the Church of Christ, and every Christian should consider it a great privilege regularly to attend its services.

He Saw the Privilege of Consecrated Service

" And straightway he preached Christ in the synagogues, that He is the Son of God." As he grew stronger in the faith, a great desire took possession of his soul. He thought of his former colleagues, and yearned to tell them the glad tidings. Enriched by his fellowship with other saints, he felt equal to the task of preaching the Gospel, and soon the Damascus synagogues echoed with the clear notes of his message. His eyes had indeed been opened, and he quickly became the example for every believer. Paul opened up the highway of Christian service, and in his footsteps we must all travel—if we are not ashamed of the Gospel of Christ.

JOHN MARK . . . the boy who made good

(ACTS 13:13; 2 TIMOTHY 4:11)

The story of John Mark is one of the most human accounts in the Bible. It tells of a young man within whose breast twin forces struggled for supremacy. Timidity and sincerity alternately urged him to action, and after a disastrous beginning, when he brought upon himself condemnation and shame, young John Mark fought back against his cruel defeat and ultimately became a famous Christian. His home was one of the first meeting places of the early Church, and it was to this house Peter made his way after his release from prison (Acts 12:12). Young John was therefore accustomed to real prayer meetings, and was fully acquainted with the power of intercession. His uncle Barnabas had become a leader of the Church, and it was he who first introduced Saul of Tarsus to the household. The young man was eager to work for the Lord, and gladly accepted the invitation to accompany the two men on the first missionary journey.

His Call

Poor John hardly knew what lay ahead. The thrills of the invitation to leave family and home disappeared when the road of service became long and difficult. Then he discovered that the important lessons of life were learned at great cost in the school of experience. Other young people envied his privilege; his mother's eyes shone with justifiable pride, and John himself stood on the mountain-top of enthusiasm and gladness. He wished people good-bye, and accompanied the two pioneers as they set sail for the dark places of the earth. Gripped by the spell of enchantment and romance, he expected to find unending inspiration in the service of Christ. Alas, it was unfortunate that almost his first journey lay over the sea.

His Collapse

" Now when Paul and his company loosed from Paphos, they came to Perga in Pamphylia: and John departing from them returned to Jerusalem." There seem to be three possibilities regarding his failure. (i) During his first sea journey he may have been sea-sick, and if that were the case, many of us can truly sympathize with him. (ii) He went forth to preach the Gospel, and instead probably spent most of his time attending to the material needs of his two leaders. When a boy has been spoiled by the unending care of a devoted mother, the sudden change to such service might easily have led to home-sickness. (iii) The future seemed dangerous and uncertain. Paul's uncompromising fearlessness would arouse the bitterness of the Jews; there would be many hardships. Perhaps Mark was a little afraid, and went home.

His Continuance

Two years later, when the boy had become a man, he was ready to go forth again; but Paul declined to have him—and this led to a quarrel with Barnabas (Acts 15:37-39). Barnabas would not give up his nephew, and Paul would not give up his convictions. They separated one from the other, and John Mark accompanied Barnabas to Cyprus. Poor lad, he was blamed for causing the great division. His inauspicious beginning had ruined his hopes of success, and it seemed that he was destined to carry for ever the stigma of failure. When Simon Peter heard of the young man's trouble, his heart was drawn to him; they had much in common. Then Mark commenced taking notes of Peter's sermons, and the collection of writings increased weekly. Soon he began to edit his material, and under the guidance of God, Mark's Gospel came into being.

His Conquest

We shall never be able to realize how hard Mark had to persevere, for it was very difficult to overcome his reputation of being a trouble maker. Yet he continued, and ultimately triumphed. Eventually even Paul was greatly impressed by what had been accomplished. Many of the Churches had refused to accept John Mark, but Paul wrote commanding them to receive the young man into fellowship (Col. 4:10). Mark's triumph was complete when Paul wrote to Timothy saying, "Take Mark, and bring him with thee: for he is profitable to me for the ministry." The great apostle who had previously refused to recognize the boy's value in the Christian ministry, now eagerly requested his services. John Mark had made good.

Dr. LUKE . . . who understudied the Great Physician

(COLOSSIANS 4:14)

The small but busy town of Troas in Asia Minor was one of the ancient gateways between east and west. The ships of the world unloaded valuable cargoes on the quayside, and in exchange carried away the produce of the inland countries. People of many nations regularly visited this thriving centre of commerce, and the need for qualified physicians increased daily. At the end of his training, Dr. Luke sought favourable opportunities in which to practise, and it appears that he chose Troas. He commenced his work, and soon the citizens became acquainted with the new doctor who had moved into their town.

The Call to Love Christ

One day a young man named Timothy called at the surgery, requesting the doctor to visit his friend Paul. As the late Dr. F. B. Meyer once suggested, the enforced march of hundreds of miles from the hinterland (Acts 16:6-8) had left the great apostle with some physical ailment, and thus Dr. Luke was provided with his opportunity to meet the untiring missionary. When the physician sought an explanation of the apparently unnecessary haste in travelling such a long journey, the patient explained the urgency of making known his message. He had been a persecutor of the faith he now loved, and had only recently been converted. He had met the risen Christ, and had dedicated his life to the ministry of the Gospel. And as Luke heard the story of the amazing Paul, his own heart was strangely stirred. Soon he also trusted the Saviour, and eventually became one of the most beloved saints of the Church.

The Call to Labour for Christ

When the doctor called to see his patient one morning, he was surprised to hear of a proposed departure. Paul had seen a vision presenting the urgency of the need of the people of Macedonia. He had therefore arranged to sail with the first boat to leave the harbour. The practised eyes of the physician easily recognized that the preacher would soon need expert help, and he resolved to accompany the party in order to serve in the same glad cause. Long afterward, when Luke wrote " The Acts of the Apostles," he described that momentous day as follows: " And after Paul had seen the vision, immediately *we* endeavoured to go into Macedonia, assuredly gathering that the Lord had called *us* for to preach the Gospel unto them " (Acts 16:10).

The Call to Learn of Christ

Within a short time Luke's premonitions were proved to be correct. The mob at Philippi assaulted the brave preacher, and thrust him into prison. When Paul was miraculously released, Dr. Luke was near at hand and attended to the wounds of his beloved colleague. Eventually the party journeyed to other centres, and each time Paul addressed a congregation, the great Dr. Luke listened attentively and increased his store of knowledge. When he began to edit his material, slowly but surely Luke's Gospel began to take shape. In addition to his many other labours, he attended to the sick of the Church, for although Paul practised the art of divine healing, there was still a place for the physician. Sometimes the Lord deliberately lays us aside in order to teach in sickness the lessons we are too busy to learn in health. The gentleness of Luke's ministry so gripped the Church that he became known as " the beloved physician." He preached with his hands while Paul preached with his voice.

The Call to Look at Christ

When Paul wrote from his prison, " Only Luke is with me " (2 Tim. 4:11), he supplied irrefutable evidence of the faithfulness of his great partner. Luke had remained loyal, and was there to superintend the funeral arrangements when his leader made the supreme sacrifice. Tradition says that he afterwards went back to spend the remaining part of his life attending to the physical needs of his brethren and sisters in Christ. He was one of the most charming saints of his age, and daily understudied the Great Physician. He adorned his faith, and fully demonstrated the attractiveness of the brotherhood of Christians. He continued until the end. He was a great man, and the Church can never have too many of his type.

FELIX . . . who played to the gallery

(ACTS 24:25-27)

The throne room was a scene of splendour and magnificence. The Governor, accompanied by his most noble lady, had taken his seat, and the illustrious assembly gathered before him prepared for the proceedings of the court. In an atmosphere of suppressed excitement, lords and ladies watched the imposing figure of Israel's high priest. That he had come voluntarily to present his case before the Governor testified eloquently to the importance of this trial. He had obtained the assistance of a foremost attorney, and the proceedings of the day promised great drama. The case for the prosecution would be pressed with the utmost urgency in the attempt to obtain judgment. The case for the defence lay in the hands of one man—the defendant. It seemed ludicrous that the best legal brains in Israel should be employed to combat the testimony of one lonely man; yet all the onlookers realized that Paul of Tarsus was no insignificant opponent. His unruffled attitude, his cloudless eyes, his fearless stance, all suggested hidden sources of confidence and power. He was a matchless orator, quick in repartee, scathing in criticism, invincible in argument. The court was hushed when the eminent counsel for the prosecution opened the case. The people could hardly fail to recognize that his phraseology exceeded his logic. He sat down. Then the prisoner arose, and a new hush descended upon the court.

The Governor Heard

Within seconds it became apparent that counsel for the defence had altered his tactics. Earlier he had faithfully reiterated the events of the period when he had been arrested, but now for some strange reason, he proceeded to speak of other matters. He seemed certain of supernatural truth, and irresistibly challenged his illustrious judge. The speech divided into three sections: (i) *God and responsibility.* The righteousness of God demanded the self-control of men. (ii) *Guilt and retribution.* All men must stand before the throne of God, to answer for the deeds done in the body. (iii) *Grace and reconciliation.* He probably explained the way by which sins could be removed and peace with God obtained. All Paul's messages followed this pattern, for he yearned to reveal to men the absolute necessity of knowing Christ. Amid subdued murmurs of astonishment the sermon ended, and even the judge could not hide his emotion. Felix looked into the challenging eyes of the prisoner, and trembled, for if this speech were authentic and reliable the future would be most unpleasant. The crowded court waited to hear the judge's summing up of the case, but their expectations were not realized.

The Governor Hesitated

He looked down at the waiting Paul and said, " Go thy way for this time; when I have a convenient season I will call for thee." And so the case was adjourned to give the judge time in which to sift the evidence. Paul returned to the cells; Felix returned to his palace, hoping that a bribe would soon be offered in exchange for the release of the prisoner. During the following months many secret inquiries were made to ascertain whether or not the prisoner had any financial backing, and each new inquiry revealed the increasing corruption of the court. The man who had once trembled before the preacher now light-heartedly postponed judgment in the endeavour to extract unlawful payment for any favour he might be disposed to show.

The Governor Hardened

Daily he increased his claim for the distinction of being one of the world's most foolish men, and in the court of universal justice will change places with his one-time prisoner. " But after two years, Porcius Festus came into Felix' room: and Felix, willing to shew the Jews a pleasure, left Paul bound." With a supercilious smile upon his face, he considered the plight of the prisoner and recalled the wishes of Israel's high priest. He shrugged his shoulders and probably laughed at the memory of his trembling, two years earlier. In the subsequent years he was remembered as the arrogant fool who loved to play to the gallery for cheap applause and popularity. Had he possessed true wisdom he would have known that even the ordinary onlookers in the gallery knew how to despise a " yes " man.

PAUL . . . at journey's end

(2 TIMOTHY 4:6, 7)

It has been said that none of the original apostles succeeded in stamping upon the infant Church the imprint of his own individuality; that this was never done before the advent of Paul. The great apostle to the Gentiles was a man of outstanding characteristics. His gifts, his untiring energy, and his ever-increasing zeal, revealed that he was the man for the moment. To him was given the inestimable privilege of carrying the Gospel message throughout the known world. The crowded market places of Asia, the proud city of Ephesus where stood the magnificent temple of Diana, the orthodox Jewish synagogues, and many other places belonged to Paul's parish; and whenever opportunity arose, the great preacher made known the mysteries of redeeming grace. Unlike others of his generation, he never turned back. Possessed by a passion to remain true to his Lord, he pressed forward, and after many years of triumphant service reached the end of his journey.

THE GREAT FIGHT. *" I have fought a good fight "*

Paul sat on his prison bench and permitted his thoughts to travel back through the years. His record of service was clearly outlined before him. In comparing his record with that of other preachers, he could say, " Are they the ministers of Christ? (I speak as a fool) I am more; in labours more abundant, in stripes above measure, in prisons more frequent, in deaths oft. Of the Jews five times received I forty stripes save one. Thrice was I beaten with rods, once was I stoned, thrice I suffered shipwreck, a night and a day I have been in the deep. . . . In weariness and painfulness, in watchings often, in hunger and thirst, in fastings often, in cold and nakedness " (2 Cor. 11 : 23-27). When Paul summed up the experiences of his lifetime he did not refer to them as if they had been a series of pleasant picnics. He had been called upon to face conflicts—hard, stern, embittered battles : and he had come through triumphantly. He had fought a good fight. The world, the flesh, and the devil had ranged themselves against him, and although on occasion he had been forced to cry "Who shall deliver me?" Christ had never failed to support him in the great hour of his need.

THE GREAT FINISH. *"I have finished my course"*

Unlike many of his former associates who had dropped out of the Christian race, Paul had continued until the end. The injunction given in Hebrews 12:1 had been faithfully observed. Deliberately he set aside every weight and the sin which so easily beset him, and ran with patience the race which was set before him. One after the other, fellow-contestants for the prize had disappeared from the course, but Paul had persevered until the prize lay within his grasp. His noble example has remained for us the greatest incentive to Christian faithfulness. Many who gave promise of greatness in the race of life disappointed their Lord, and forgot His word, "Be not weary in well doing, for in due season we shall reap if we faint not." Alas, so many humans are like a vessel stranded and helpless in the shallow waters of a rocky beach.

THE GREAT FAITH. *"I have kept the faith"*

Perhaps this was the highlight of Paul's statement. The new message had been entrusted to his care. He spoke about "my Gospel," and through all the changing scenes of life he had faithfully preached the story of redeeming grace. He had met the risen Saviour, and even those people who denied the truth of his declarations could not fail to recognize the unswerving loyalty of the indomitable missionary. Now, at journey's end, he was ready to go home to heaven. The Greek word translated "departure" has a twofold meaning—to be released; and to go on a journey. Death had no terrors for Paul. He had long known the desire to be released from his tabernacle of flesh (Phil. 1:23), but until now his wish had not been granted. At last the ambitions of his heart are to be realized. He will soon leave his earthly body and start upon his last great journey. Triumphantly he cried, "Henceforth there is laid up for me a crown." He calmly awaited the coming of the executioner whose axe would effectively open his door of escape. When the moment came he had a great "Welcome Home," and probably all heaven smiled when the Lord said, "Well done, thou good and faithful servant." He deserved it! Shall I?

PETER . . . who fell in love with a word

It is sometimes surprising how a single word may be able to express great intensity of feeling. Many men and women who have been deeply stirred by outstanding events instinctively choose the strongest adjectives, and even then feel their utterances are inadequate. Simon Peter was a man of varying moods. He had known the mountain-tops and also the valleys of human experience. Supreme joy had been followed by abject despair; yet through all the changing fortunes of his discipleship he had known the constancy of his Lord's kindness. When Peter became an old man his sacred reminiscences were expressed in two epistles, and in both these letters he betrays his love for the word " precious."

The Precious Blood of Christ

" Forasmuch as ye know that ye were not redeemed with corruptible things, as silver and gold . . . but with the precious blood of Christ, as of a lamb without blemish and without spot " (1 Peter 1:18, 19). Perhaps it is very fitting that this should represent Peter's first use of the word. As an orthodox Jew he had been acquainted with the practice of offering a half-shekel of silver as atonement money for his soul. Peter now realized that the Old Testament types had been fulfilled in Christ; that redemption had been provided through the Lamb of God. It is worthy of consideration that nowhere in the Old Testament is the blood of the offering referred to as " the precious blood." Christ superseded all that had ever gone before.

The Precious Corner Stone

" Behold, I lay in Sion a chief corner stone, elect, precious: and he that believeth in Him shall not be confounded. Unto you therefore which believe *he is precious* " (1 Peter 2:6, 7). Peter recognized that the Gospel had changed everything. The importance of the priesthood of all believers far exceeded the levitical order. Even the grandeur of the temple was now of little importance, for the fellowship of saints had created another dwelling in which true fellowship and worship would be pre-eminent.

165

Behind the corner stone Peter found shelter from the storms of life. *In the corner stone* he found the strength that united and linked the other living stones of the spiritual temple. *Upon the corner stone* he found the confidence with which he and all others could rest in safety. Christ fully met the need of His Church. He was very precious!

The Precious Faith

" Simon Peter, a servant and an apostle of Jesus Christ, to them that have obtained like precious faith with us " (2 Peter 1:1). As Peter grew in grace he realized that the Gospel of Christ included much more than reconciliation to God. It was very wonderful to be brought nigh to God by the power of the cross, but through the merits of the Saviour the one-time enemy would be transformed into the likeness of God's Son. Grace and peace obtained through Christ at conversion could be *multiplied* through the soul's increasing knowledge of God and the Saviour. In every conceivable way the new faith superseded the old one. The traditions of the fathers had been swept aside by the intimacy of this union with the Godhead. The Gospel was not for the privileged few, but for all the people in the world. It was indeed a precious faith.

The Precious Promises

" According as His divine power hath given unto us all things that pertain unto life and godliness, through the knowledge of Him that hath called us to glory and virtue: Whereby are given unto us *exceeding great and precious promises*" (2 Peter 1:3, 4). Simon Peter could not foresee all the future details of his life, but he remained calm in the confidence that God's promises were true and faithful. They met every phase of human need. The Lord's promise, " I will never leave thee, nor forsake thee," was music for his soul; and every time he set out on a journey he recalled his Master's words, "Lo, I am with you alway." The promises of God were most wonderful, and it was not really surprising that he described them as " exceeding great and precious."

The apostle was a great human, and fully demonstrated the fact that the Spirit of God can lift a man above his failures in order to make him an instrument of blessing to countless thousands of people.

THE REDEEMED . . . and how they reached home
(REVELATION 7:14)

The Bible begins with the sad account of man being thrust out from the garden and from the immediate presence of God. It ends with the fact of his being brought into an eternal home, nevermore to be separated from his heavenly Father. It is a long story from the beginning to the end. Man's redemption was not accomplished in a moment. It seems a long way from the garden to the glory; and although Jacob's ladder once spanned the distance, alas, the travellers upon it were too select for the company of a poor sinner. Another way had to be found, so that a wayfaring man though a fool would not err therein. Thus in His eternal counsels the Almighty planned a Cross. John in the final episode of Holy Writ has much to say of this, and of the people who through its message reached home. Perhaps the greatest of all his utterances is found in Revelation 7. He wrote of the redeemed: " These are they who have washed their robes, and made them white in the blood of the Lamb."

Here is Cleansing Provided by God

This is *the blood of the Lamb.* The Old Testament never speaks of the *precious* blood. The way of escape provided by the law was not eternally effective, but rather a temporary measure destined to bring relief. The word used for " atonement " simply means " to cover." Sins were not banished but hidden. The Lamb of God came to take them away for ever. That God had endeavoured to prepare His people for this great truth is clear, since all Old Testament typology points to it. The offering of Abel was accepted because it was a lamb of the flock. Isaac was rescued from the altar because an offering took his place. Israel in Egypt escaped judgment because the blood of the Lamb stood between them and retribution. The daily ministrations in the temple taught that man could only be accepted through the blood of an offering; and if any climax were needed to the long list of illustrations, the thrilling announcement of John Baptist would provide it—" Behold the Lamb of God. which taketh away the sins of the world." This is something provided by God.

Here is Cleansing Accepted by Man

" *They have washed* their robes." John implies three suggestive truths. (i) The people who washed their robes surely recognized that the robes needed to be cleansed. They would hardly wash robes which were spotless. (ii) These people knew where cleansing could be obtained. Somehow they had discovered the great fountain-head of all blessing. (iii) The greatest fact of all is that *they washed* their robes. Many people are convinced of the truth of points one and two, and yet postpone action. Here, at least, faith without works is dead. If a man knows his need of Christ, he must act accordingly and come to Christ; otherwise his knowledge only increases his condemnation.

Here is Cleansing Recognized by Heaven

" These are they who have washed their robes . . . therefore are they before the throne of God." John is careful in pointing out that these people are not anticipating heaven—they are already there. However difficult the crossing from sin to sublimity, the rigours of the way have all been overcome. These people are home, and not because they were eminent citizens emanating virtue, but rather because they washed their robes and made them white in the blood of the Lamb. Guilty and undeserving of mercy, they had bowed at the throne of grace. They had not done so in vain. "And they sung a new song, saying, Thou art worthy . . . for thou wast slain, and hast redeemed us to God by thy blood out of every kindred, and tongue, and people, and nation . . . and the number of them was ten thousand times ten thousand, and thousands of thousands." Command Performance! I must be sure to be there.

HINTS FOR THE YOUNG PREACHER

The work of preaching the Gospel is the noblest calling in the world, and for that reason all who are privileged to share this great honour should endeavour to increase their efficiency in the presentation of the message. The realization that much might be at stake will assist in deepening the desire to present the Gospel in the best possible way. A home might be saved from ruin, a life saved from eternal sorrow, and above all else, the Lord Jesus may be glorified, if the preacher can succeed in implanting his words in the hearts of his listeners. It is therefore imperative that he who preaches the Gospel should do his job well. And with this, as with everything else in life, there is a right and wrong way of approaching the task. The man who excuses his laziness and inefficiency by saying " I have only to open my mouth and God will fill it," forgets that other agencies might fill his mouth before God gets a chance! Such men generally succeed in advertising their own stupidity. This chapter is not meant to be an authority on the subject of homiletics, but rather to provide help for the young minister who finds difficulty in his weekly routine of sermon preparation. The itinerant preacher has less strain than the settled pastor, for his messages can often be repeated. The man who preaches to the same people week after week, generally discovers that the task of preparing new messages can be very difficult. This book, and particularly this chapter, is a sincere attempt to offer assistance to all such young ministers.

1. *Endeavour to preach without notes*

I have often repeated this to the divinity classes in various colleges, and without exception have seen frowns of worry and despair immediately appearing upon the faces of the students. All men are not gifted alike. Some have excellent memories, while others, lacking in self-confidence, are left to struggle along with the help of copious notes. Nevertheless, the young preacher should endeavour to reach the place where his written sermon will be unnecessary. He will certainly not reach this standard of efficiency in a moment, but he should undoubtedly make this his ultimate ambition; for whatever arguments may be advanced against this advice, one thing remains indisputable. The preacher who is able to look into the faces of his audience has a far better chance of capturing their attention than the man whose eyes are always upon his notes. At the best of times people are strange beings, but in fairness to them let it be said that it is seldom pleasant to listen to a man who reads on and on and on. If the preacher can read his text, look up at his listeners, and proceed to deliver his message in a manly and business-like way, he will immediately see appreciative interest shining in the eyes of his congregation. Every young minister should therefore endeavour to reach the place where notes will not be indispensable. This may not be difficult if he approaches the task in the correct way.

2. *Avoid repetition, and be natural*

We must never under-estimate the greatness of our calling, and with dignity befitting our profession must adorn the Gospel we preach. Nevertheless it is well to remember that we are still men, and true manhood has always been the object of a world's admiration. I shall never forget a night in Northern Rhodesia when I stood in a hall filled with miners. I had been sent there by the Baptist Union of South Africa in order to hold special evangelistic services. There was neither pulpit nor platform in the hall, and since I am but a modest five feet seven inches in height, I could not see the burly faces at the back of the crowded meeting place. I assumed that they also had difficulty in seeing me. When I offered to stand upon the table, one rough miner said, " Yes, sir, please do." Afterward he said to his friends, " He's not like a parson. He's a man—he's like us." I considered that to be my greatest compliment. There is no one so absurd as the man who enters a pulpit immediately to become another fellow whose attitude, voice, and demeanour are totally foreign from those of his natural life. We must remember that God made us to be ourselves, and not to copy other people. Let us be natural, and endeavour in our preaching to avoid needless repetition. When we enter the pulpit we should know exactly the line of thought along which we intend to take our listeners. In most nonconformist churches the people expect a thirty-minute sermon.

Sometimes according to the taste of the members, twenty minutes are sufficient, but in other centres—especially Wales—the " big meeting " calls for an oration of one hour's duration. Unless the message has been carefully prepared, the speaker is likely to discover after fifteen minutes that he has exhausted his stock of information. It is a terrible feeling to look at the clock, to know one has to continue for another ten or fifteen minutes, and to realize one has nothing left to say. The speaker by a circumlocution then returns to his earlier remarks and repeats what he has already said. The avoidance of this error should be his first consideration.

3. *Make a clearly defined outline*

What scaffolding is to a house, headings are to a sermon. They are.helps in the work of erection. When the house is finished the scaffolding disappears. This is not strictly true concerning a sermon, for sometimes the retention of the main points of the discourse will help in fastening the message upon the walls of memory. Nevertheless, true importance rests in the message and not in the outline. The headings are only there to assist the preacher in formulating his ideas. For example, should there be three clearly defined points, and should the preacher be able to spend five minutes in dealing with each of these, he has already fifteen minutes of his message. If he prefaces point one with an interesting introduction, and then follows the third point with a vital climax in the form of a telling illustration, he has every chance of preaching for twenty-five minutes without fear of having to repeat himself. The main examples included in " Bible Cameos " will illustrate what is meant by this statement. Sometimes the Biblical story has been divided; at other times the text has been divided; and on occasion several Scriptures have been grouped together. This has been deliberately done in order to illustrate the fact that no preacher should ever allow himself to get into a rut. The introduction should be planned to gain the undivided attention of the audience. While this is being done, the speaker finds comfort in the fact that his first heading is ready. When he has dealt with this, he can proceed to his second point, and thus in orderly measured fashion can develop the theme. In this way also the hearers can appreciate the clarity of the speaker's thought. Points one, two, and three should be leading toward a definite climax. When the preacher has completed his message, the listeners should be face to face with the Lord Jesus, and the appeal should be made for personal decision. If the congregation disperses saying, " What a wonderful preacher," the speaker has failed in his mission. If the people have been moved to say, " What a wonderful Saviour," he should get on his knees and thank God he has been able to fulfil the greatest requirements of the Christian ministry. The matter of outline is of supreme importance, but no one should try to be clever in creating startling headings. For example, let me quote the man who preached about the prodigal son. His three points were—1 . . . Packing the togs. 2 . . . Feeding the hogs. 3 . . . Going to the dogs. Such stupidity would make a street-corner crowd laugh, but would offend the worshippers in any house of God. The outline of the sermon should be sane, healthy, and attractive.

4. *Wisely choose your illustrations*

I have already likened the sermon to a house. Let me now say that the illustrations are the windows of the house. A window out of all proportion to the size of the house makes the entire structure appear comical, and in just the same manner, lengthy illustrative stories may ruin the sermon. Many young ministers have difficulty in obtaining suitable illustrations, and to them I commend the group system as found in some of the chapters of this book. The Bible is rich in illustrative values, and oftentimes one story can perfectly illustrate a point of another. No effort should be spared in seeking additional helps, but in emergency the Bible stories will be the best treasure house.

5. *Carefully prepare your introduction*

This is most important, for every person in the congregation will readily listen for two minutes. I shall always be indebted to Professor Garvey for his statement in regard to the introductions of sermons. In the early days of my preaching, his essay revealed to me the great necessity of capturing the attention of the audience during those initial moments. After the third hymn, and immediately before the sermon, the people will sit down, make themselves moderately comfortable, cough once or twice and then look expectantly toward the preacher, as if to say, " Now what will he be like?" If he is not very interesting, the women may begin thinking about a knitting pattern, and the men wonder what kind of opposition might be forthcoming in the next bowling match! The congregation will be present in body but absent in thought. Let us test ourselves. Have we not sat in a congregation and felt ashamed of our inability to prevent our thoughts wandering? The same thing might happen to our hearers unless we can hold them right from the beginning of the message. Those first two minutes are exceedingly important. A well-chosen question, a problem, or even a little laughter might work wonders, for once the attention of the hearers has been gained it will be easy to retain it afterward.

6. *Be sure that your own heart has been well prepared*

Dr. Jowett once said, " A minister's study should be an upper room and not a lounge." Every experienced preacher will readily admit that a flurried or unclean heart will hinder the effectiveness of his message. Before we go to stand before the faces of our people, we should look into the face of our Lord. It was said of the first New Testament preacher: " There was a man sent from God whose name was John." And that should be true of all who stand in the holy place. Unless we come forth fresh from the presence of the Most High we shall have little chance of gripping the consciences of the Lord's people. If we have lingered in the divine Presence, if we have gazed into eternal beauty, we shall come forth " with the skin of our faces shining," and our listeners will know we have been with God. The prepared heart is even more necessary than the prepared sermon, for " though I speak with the tongues of men and of angels, and have not love, I am become as sounding brass, or a tingling cymbal." We must remember when we go forth to tell the story of redeeming love that every angel would gladly exchange places with us. Ours is the greatest privilege in the world. Let us approach the task with fortitude and courage, refusing to be discouraged, and determined by God's help to be proficient in winning men for Christ.

INDEX

Combined and Comprehensive Bible Index Covering Bible Cameos—Bible Pinnacles—Bible Treasures

GENESIS:						PAGE
1:26	...	B. Treasures	...	...	...	114
2:8-9	...	B. Pinnacles	...	...	...	19
2:21-22	...	B. Pinnacles	...	...	...	1
3:10	...	B. Cameos	...	...	...	1
3:22	...	B. Cameos	...	...	...	131
3:22-24	...	B. Pinnacles	...	...	...	19
3:24	...	B. Pinnacles	...	...	...	6
4:1-10	...	B. Pinnacles	...	...	...	3
4:16-26	...	B. Treasures	...	...	...	1
5:21-22	...	B. Treasures	...	...	...	3
5:24	...	B. Pinnacles	...	...	...	5
6:20	...	B. Cameos	...	...	...	3
7:10	...	B. Pinnacles	...	...	...	167
9:4	...	B. Treasures	...	...	...	145
9:13	...	B. Pinnacles	...	...	...	168
13:1-4	...	B. Cameos	...	...	...	5
13:7-18	...	B. Treasures	...	...	...	5
18:9-15	...	B. Pinnacles	...	...	...	7
18:27	...	B. Treasures	...	...	...	7
19:16-22	...	B. Cameos	...	...	...	7
19:17	...	B. Treasures	...	...	...	9
19:26	...	B. Treasures	...	...	...	9
21:5	...	B. Pinnacles	...	...	...	9
21:14-19	...	B. Cameos	...	...	...	130
22:5	...	B. Pinnacles	...	...	...	9
22:8	...	B. Pinnacles	...	...	...	10
22:15-18	...	B. Pinnacles	...	...	...	10
24:1-10	...	B. Pinnacles	...	...	...	11
24:58-67	...	B. Pinnacles	...	...	...	11
25:21	...	B. Pinnacles	...	...	...	12
25:29-34	...	B. Cameos	...	...	...	11
26:18	...	B. Cameos	...	...	...	9
27:38	...	B. Cameos	...	...	...	12
28:2-11	...	B. Pinnacles	...	...	...	13
28:10-17	...	B. Pinnacles	...	...	...	13
32:24-35	...	B. Cameos	...	...	...	13
37:41	...	B. Cameos	...	...	...	15
50:25	...	B. Treasures	...	...	...	11

EXODUS:						
3:4	...	B. Treasures	...	...	...	13
3:13-14	...	B. Treasures	...	...	...	122

179

189

BOOKS BY IVOR POWELL

BIBLE GEMS

Mini-messages with an ample supply of sermon starters, illustrations and deep truths from God's Word.

ISBN 0-8254-3527-7   176 pp.   paperback

BIBLE HIGHWAYS

Scripture texts are linked together, suggesting highways through the Bible from Genesis to Revelation.

ISBN 0-8254-3521-8   176 pp.   paperback

BIBLE NAMES OF CHRIST

80 short studies on the names and titles of the Lord Jesus Christ. The simplicity and freshness of these mini-messages will provide enlightening devotional studies for believers and many outlines for teachers and preachers.

ISBN 0-8254-3530-7   176 pp.   paperback

BIBLE PINNACLES

A spiritual adventure into the lives and miracles of Bible characters and the meaningful parables of our Lord.

ISBN 0-8254-3516-1   192 pp.   paperback

BIBLE TREASURES

In refreshingly different style and presentation, these 80 Bible miracles and parables are vividly portrayed.

ISBN 0-8254-3518-8   182 pp.   paperback

BIBLE WINDOWS

Anecdotes and stories are, in fact, windows through which the Gospel light shines, to illumine lessons for preachers.

ISBN 0-8254-3522-6   180 pp.   paperback

DAVID: HIS LIFE AND TIMES

David, the "sweet Psalmist of Israel," comes alive in the unique and refreshing manner typical of Ivor Powell's writings.

ISBN 0-8254-3523-3   416 pp.   paperback

MATTHEW'S MAJESTIC GOSPEL

You will find almost everything you need in developing sermons: theme, outline, expository notes, preaching homilies.

ISBN 0-8254-3525-0   526 pp.   hardback

MARK'S SUPERB GOSPEL

This most systematic study offers expositional, devotional and homiletical thoughts with alliterated outlines.

ISBN 0-8254-3523-4   432 pp.   hardback

LUKE'S THRILLING GOSPEL

In this practical and perceptive commentary, there is a gold-mine of expository notes and homilies.

ISBN 0-8254-3513-7   508 pp.   hardback

JOHN'S WONDERFUL GOSPEL

Another verse-by-verse, distinctively different commentary with sermonic notes and outlines.

ISBN 0-8254-3514-5   446 pp.   hardback

THE AMAZING ACTS

The Acts of the Apostles become relevant for today in this most helpful exposition.

ISBN 0-8254-3526-9   478 pp.   hardback

THE EXCITING EPISTLE TO THE EPHESIANS

The book of Ephesians comes alive in this insightful, verse-by-verse exposition of one of Paul's most important Epistles.

ISBN 0-8254-3537-4   304 pp.   hardback

WHAT IN THE WORLD WILL HAPPEN NEXT?

An unusual work on prophecy dealing especially with the return of Christ to earth and the nation of Israel's future.

ISBN 0-8254-3524-2   176 pp.   paperback

Available at your local Christian bookseller, or:

KREGEL Publications

P. O. Box 2607 • Grand Rapids, MI 49501-2607